YOU WERE
MADE TO
MAKE A
DIFFERENCE

YOU WERE MADE TO MAKE A DIFFERENCE

MAX LUCADO
AND JENNA LUCADO BISHOP

WITH NATALIE GILLESPIE

Tommy NELSON®

A Division of Thomas Nelson Publishers

NASHVILLE · MEXICO CITY · RIO DE JANEIRO

You Were Made to Make a Difference

© 2010 by Max Lucado

Published in Nashville, Tennessee, by Tommy Nelson®. Tommy Nelson is a trademark of Thomas Nelson, Inc.

Thomas Nelson, Inc., titles may be purchased in bulk for educational, business, fund-raising, or sales promotional use. For information, please e-mail SpecialMarkets@ThomasNelson.com.

Unless otherwise noted, Scripture quotations are taken from the New Century Version®. © 2005 by Thomas Nelson, Inc. Used by permission. All rights reserved.

Scripture quotations marked NIV are taken from the Holy Bible: New International Version,® NIV. © 1973, 1978, 1984 by Biblica, Inc. Used by permission of Zondervan. All rights reserved.

Scripture quotations marked NLT are taken from *Holy Bible*, New Living Translation. © 1996, 2004. Used by permission of Tyndale House Publishers, Inc., Wheaton, Illinois 60189. All rights reserved.

Scripture quotations marked CEV are taken from The Contemporary English Version. © 1991 by the American Bible Society. Used by permission.

Scripture quotations marked MSG are taken from The Message by Eugene H. Peterson. © 1993, 1994, 1995, 1996, 2000. Used by permission of NavPress Publishing Group. All rights reserved.

Scripture quotations marked NKJV are taken from The New King James Version. © 1982 by Thomas Nelson, Inc. Used by permission. All rights reserved.

One hundred percent of the author's royalties from *Outlive Your Life* products will benefit children and families through World Vision and other ministries of faith-based compassion. To follow World Vision's use of the funds, go to MaxLucado.com.

Photographs marked ©Jon Warren/World Vision 2010 are used by permission of World Vision.

Quotes marked ML are by Max Lucado.

All photographs used by permission.

Library of Congress Cataloging-in-Publication Data

Lucado, Max.
    You were made to make a difference/Max Lucado and Jenna Lucado Bishop with Natalie Gillespie.
        p. cm.
    Adaptation of: Lucado, Max. Outlive your life.
    Includes bibliographical references (p.).
    ISBN 978-1-4003-1600-7 (softcover)
1. Christian teenagers—Religious life. 2. Christian life. I. Bishop, Jenna Lucado. II. Gillespie, Natalie Nichols. III. Lucado, Max. Outlive your life. IV. Title.
    BV4531.3.L83133 2010
    248.4—dc22   2010018907

Printed in the United States of America

15 16 17 18 RRD 15 14

Mfr.: RRD/Crawfordsville/USA/November 2015/ PO#9374786

Dedicated to the children of the Oak Hills' missionaries. You are making a difference!

CONTENTS

Acknowledgments   ix

A Note from the Authors   x

Don't Just Breathe—Live!   xiii

PART 1: YOU WERE MADE TO BELONG TO GOD

1. Good Morning, Life   3
2. Plain Cheese Pizza   21
3. No Dropped Calls   39
4. Hidden Treasure   53

PART 2: YOU WERE MADE TO REACH OUT TO OTHERS

5. Unplug and Tune In   73
6. 20/20   89
7. Stand Up for the Have-Nots   103
8. When to Put Up Your Dukes   125

PART 3: YOU WERE MADE TO CHANGE THE WORLD

9. When a Whole Generation Says Go!   141
10. Hang Out Your Welcome Sign   161
11. Blast the Walls Down   177
12. How to Make a Difference Every Day   191

Random Acts of Kindness and Good Deeds   201

Notes   207

ACKNOWLEDGMENTS

Bravo to Laura Minchew, Beverly Phillips, June Ford, Jennifer Stair, Dawn Woods, Patti Evans, Lori Lynch, and the rest of the Tommy Nelson team for shepherding this book from concept to reality.

And a standing "O" for writer Natalie Gillespie, who did a masterful job of adapting the ideas and stories from *Outlive Your Life* into the language of teens. We're grateful.

A NOTE FROM THE AUTHORS

> You
> were made
> to be
> a world-changer.
> **Yes, you!**

God created every person on this earth with a special purpose—and the world is waiting for you to share yours! Don't let your youth hold you back.

Max

Whether young or old, everyone can make a difference for good. Speaking a kind word, volunteering time, donating items, raising money for nonprofits—the ways to make a difference are limitless. My prayer is that this book helps you discover the many ways you can use your God-given gifts to make a difference that outlives your life. In the pages that follow, you'll see not only the incredible changes brought about by first-century Christians, but also what young people just like you are doing today.

Jenna

I had the pure privilege to piggyback on the vision God gave my dad for this book. And I am honored to come along for the ride. We want you to know, first and foremost, that God loves you. And it is only through his love that you can love others, serve others, and even change the world. So will you make a decision right now to open your heart up to his life-changing love? Because I can promise you now, when it hits, it hits hard! And before you know it, God will start using you. Yes, YOU! No matter where you are or where you have been, God wants to use your story to change the world. After all, he *made* you to make a difference.

DON'T JUST BREATHE—LIVE!

 JENNA

Hey, I gotta "duh" comment for you.

You are alive.

"Wow, Jenna, so profound," you may be thinking with some slight sarcasm.

No, but let's think about it. I don't know about you, but a lot of times I forget that I'm breathing, I forget that my heart is beating. I forget life is a gift. If you are alive (which, I'm guessing you are if you are reading this right now), what are you doing about it? Are you pouring life into a flat screen, a trendy store, a sport, a phone, an unhealthy relationship? Want to make something of your life? Well, then read this next comment.

God is alive.

No sarcasm allowed after this comment. I don't want to hear any "duhs." Why? Because if we really, I mean REALLY, believed this statement, then our lives probably wouldn't look the way they do now. There would be less insecurity, less self-ishness, less laziness, less media consumption, less confusion.

See, when we experience a relationship with a LIVING God, then we begin LIVING godly. Our actions, decisions, words, dreams all change. In a good way! We live with confidence, selflessness, motivation, relationships, and purpose. When we get to know this God who loves us inside and out, then we begin to change from the inside out. We begin living for what we were made to do: Make a Difference!

PART 1

YOU WERE MADE TO BELONG TO GOD

I
I WAS MADE
I WAS MADE
TO MAKE
I WAS MADE
TO MAKE A
DIFFERENCE!

God = L♥ve

I can do all things
through Christ,
because he gives
me strength.
(Philippians 4:13)

I am God's
masterpiece!

Change
the
world
one deed
at a time.

Smile.
It's contagious!

CHAPTER 1

GOOD MORNING, LIFE

No eye has seen, no ear has heard,
no mind has conceived what God has prepared
for those who love him.

1 Corinthians 2:9 NIV

How'd your morning go?

Your alarm went off, and you hummed as your feet hit the floor, cheerfully cleaned up the bathroom after you used it, and said "Good morning" to God as you read your Bible. You ate a perfectly balanced breakfast and unloaded the dishwasher, then kissed your parents before sailing out the door for school. Right?

Eggs have thirteen vitamins and minerals and contain the highest quality food protein known. One hen produces 300 to 325 eggs a year.

—GoodEgg.com

So not right. Probably not even close.

Maybe your morning went more like this:

"Get up! I've already called you three times," your mom said. "You're gonna be late!"

"Coming," you mumbled, then rolled over and put the pillow over your head. After two or three more unsuccessful tries, your mother finally sent your little brother to get you. You chucked the pillow at him and ordered him out of your room, then staggered into the bathroom to eliminate bed head and the fuzz on your teeth. Twenty minutes later, you ducked your chores as you hurried through the kitchen, grabbing a Pop-Tart on your way out the door and barely acknowledging any of your family members.

Sound more like it?

Okay, maybe you weren't that bad.

But answer this, honestly: did you wake up today with that butterflies-in-the-stomach feeling that something great was about to happen, and you had a leading role in it? You know the one. It's the feeling you got as a little kid when you were going to Disney World or when Christmas was coming the next day.

Here's a little-known secret:

You can wake up wonder-filled
if you know that something
wonderful
is about to happen.

Especially when you discover that the key to something wonderful is *you*.

Yes, you.

MAX |||||||||||||||||||||||||||||||||||||||||||||||||||||||||||||||||||||||||||||||||||||||||||||||||||||||||||

You see, you've already walked and talked, smelled crayons and swung bats, gurgled and giggled your way out of diapers and into childhood.

> You've noticed how guys aren't girls
> and dogs aren't cats
> and pizza sure beats spinach.
> That's life. And this one is yours.

Complete with summers and songs and gray skies and tears, you have a life. Didn't ask for one, but you have one. A first day. A final day. And a few thousand in-between. You've been given an honest-to-goodness human life. Not only that, but you've been given *your* life. No one else has your version. You'll never bump into yourself on the sidewalk. Your life will never be lived by anyone else. You're not a hoodie in an attic that can be recycled after you are gone.

Some people don't think about stuff like this. But you aren't one of them. Or you wouldn't be holding a book called *You Were Made to Make a Difference*. You want your life to matter. You want to wake up excited every day. You want to live in such a way that the world will be glad you did. Like Father Benjamin. Consider his tale.

FINDING FATHER BENJAMIN: A FABLE

Strong winds blow a ship off course, and sailors spot uncharted islands. They see half a dozen mounds rising up

continued »

out of the blue South Sea waters. The captain orders the men to set anchor and goes ashore.

On the first island, he sees nothing but sadness. Underfed children. Tribes in conflict. No farming or food development, no treatment for the sick, no schools. Just simple, needy people.

The second and following islands show more of the same. The captain sighs at what he sees. "This is no life for these people." But what can he do?

Then he steps onto the last and largest island. The people are healthy and well fed. Irrigation systems water their fields and roads connect the villages. The children have bright eyes and strong bodies. The captain asks the chief for an explanation. How has this island moved so far ahead of the others?

The chief gives a quick response: "Father Benjamin. He educated us in everything from agriculture to health. He built schools and clinics and dug wells."

The captain asks, "Can you take me to see him?"

The chief nods and signals for two tribesmen to join him. They guide the captain over a jungle ridge to a medical clinic. It is equipped with clean beds and staffed with trained caretakers. They show the captain the shelves of medicine and introduce him to the staff. The captain, though impressed, sees nothing of Father Benjamin. He repeats his request. "I would like to see Father Benjamin. Can you take me to where he lives?"

The three natives look puzzled. They talk among themselves. After several minutes, the chief invites, "Follow us to the other side of the island." They walk along the shoreline until they reach a series of fishponds. Canals connect the ponds to the ocean. As the tide rises, fish pass from the ocean into the ponds. The islanders then lower canal gates and trap the fish for harvest.

Again the captain is amazed. He meets fishermen and workers, gatekeepers and net casters. But he sees nothing of Father Benjamin. He wonders if he is making himself clear.

"I don't see Father Benjamin. Please take me to where he lives."

The trio talks among themselves again. After some discussion the chief offers, "Let's go up the mountain." They lead the captain up a steep, narrow path. After many twists and turns the path deposits them in front of a grass-roofed chapel. The voice of the chief is soft and earnest. "He has taught us about God."

He escorts the captain inside and shows him the altar, a large wooden cross, several rows of benches, and a Bible.

"Is this where Father Benjamin lives?" the captain asks.

The men nod and smile.

"May I talk to him?'

Their faces grow suddenly serious. "Oh, that would be impossible."

"Why?'

"He died many years ago."

The confused captain stares at the men. "I asked to see him and you showed me a clinic, some fish farms, and this chapel. You said nothing of his death."

"You didn't ask about his death," the chief explains. "You asked to see where he lives. We showed you."

Father Benjamin made a difference that outlasted his own life.

So can you. You're not quite an adult yet. You still have a lot to learn. But God is ready to work through you now to change the world. And when you sign up for God's grand adventure, there's nothing you two can't do.

JENNA ～～～～～～～～～～～～～～～～～～～～～～～

How do I know? I've seen it in action.
Watched teens making a difference.
Even teens who had very little to work with.
Back up.
Rewind.

Let me introduce myself (in case you skipped the introduction). I'm Jenna, and you just heard from my dad. (Well, I call him Dad . . . Daddy-O . . . dork.) But no matter what I call him, there's one way I describe my dad: real. Just a real guy, with real dreams, real bad dance moves, and a real passion for Jesus.

Dad's passion for God stirs his passion for people. And as cheesy as this sounds, I want to be just like him. We wrote this book to get you excited about going on an awesome adventure with God. So that you can make a BIG difference in this world full of hurting and hungry people.

Dad and I had the privilege of visiting Ethiopia with World Vision. We saw poverty, tasted drought, touched children with AIDS . . . yet heard them sing. Sing! With joy! We watched them serve. With joy! In the midst of their disease and hunger, they sang. Why? They know a God who loves them and has a BIG purpose for their lives. They made a difference in me.

Here's Dad and my mom in Ethiopia with the little girl they sponsor.

That's me in the middle, surrounded by students at Adulala Kochore Primary School in Ethiopia. See their smiles?

I want to be like my dad.

I want to be like the Ethiopians.

I want to make a difference.

Do you?

We hope you do. And we want to help you get started. Wherever you are, you've got something to offer.

You may not think it's much.

But God does.

He made **you.**

He made you **one-of-a-kind.**

He made you to make a **difference.**

You were custom-crafted by a God who is head over heels for you. God carefully, adoringly put you together with a unique combination of personality, skills, talents, feelings, and looks. He designed you differently from anybody else on this great, big blue ball called Earth. He handcrafted every strand of hair on your head. Painstakingly painted your irises blue, green, or brown. Programmed your brain to be pretty good at math or a whiz in history. Then he stepped back, looked you over, and smiled as he pronounced his creation "good."

IRIS: *The colored part of your eye. Your pupil is in the middle of it.*

JENNA

But let's get honest. How do you see yourself? Go ahead, stand in front of the closest mirror and check yourself out.

Where do your eyes drift first? That Cyclops zit on your forehead, the new haircut that Mom loves and you hate, that body that needs more muscle or less chub? I don't know about you, but I typically focus on the flaw instead of stand in awe. If only we could see ourselves through God's eyes.

When God sees you, he cannot help but smile and sigh with satisfaction. *What a masterpiece!* he must think. *I made no mistake when I breathed her into existence or when I knit him together.* He sees a work of art more valuable than any Leonardo da Vinci at the Louvre.

When I was in eighth grade, I had to make my first-ever explosive volcano for earth science class. My partner and I spent hours forming and molding it, painting it just the right colors and, of course, making sure it could do what we made it to do—erupt! We were so proud of that creation.

Oh, the pride God has as our Father when he stands back and looks at us after molding and shaping our hearts, coloring our hair just the right shade of brown. Filling in our eyes with the perfect shade of hazel. Dusting our faces with freckles, dimples, and smile wrinkles. But it's up to us to decide whether we will do what he created us to do—know his love for us and love him in return.

When we live out this purpose, then and ONLY then can we live a life of meaning, a life that changes other lives, a life that is beyond ourselves. It's a life partnered with God to change the world.

Picture God on his heavenly throne, surrounded by angels, bursting at the seams with joy as he looks down at you. Not just on the adorable baby you were on the day you were born, but right now. Today. God is singing over you.

God loves you so much that he made you to worship him. He sent his son Jesus to die for you so that you can give your life back to him. So you can fall in love with him. And when you do, he has adventures planned that only the two of you can take. Wonderful things for you to discover. Ways that you and he can change the world.

It's in Christ that we find out who we are and what we are living for.
(Ephesians 1:11 MSG)

He will rejoice over you. You will rest in his love; he will sing and be joyful about you.
(Zephaniah 3:17)

We are created by a great God to do great works. He invites us to outlive our lives, not just in heaven, but here on earth. —ML

Yep, there's no doubt about it.

YOU WERE MADE TO MAKE A DIFFERENCE!

MADE *(adj.)*: 1. *put together of various ingredients*; 2. *assured of success*
(Merriam-Webster.com)

We are God's masterpiece. He has created us anew in Christ Jesus, so we can do the good things he planned for us long ago.
(Ephesians 2:10 NLT)

DIFFERENCE = *the answer to a subtraction problem, like the difference of 16 − 4 = 12.*

Uh, back up. Rewind again. Not the math kind of difference. The . . .

MAKE-THE-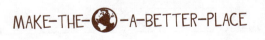-A-BETTER-PLACE

kind of difference.

Not after you go to college or get a job.

(Right now.)

Not after you finish algebra or
graduate high school.

(Right now!)

It's never too soon—and you're never too
young—to start making a difference.

RIGHT NOW!!

You,
changing lives,
changing your family,
changing your community,
changing hearts,
with the God who made the universe.
The God who made *you*. The God who wants to be your
  loving Father.

And when you make that kind of difference with him, you
can't wait to wake up and do it again. And again. And again.
Every day.

JENNA ～～～～～～～～～～～～～～～～～～～～～～～～～

Have you looked into the eyes of a homeless woman and listened to her story?

Have you held the hand of a sad friend?

Have you surprised your mom by cleaning the kitchen?

When I serve, I feel joy, excitement, satisfaction. Why? Because I'm living in my calling.

When you serve others, you serve God. And when you serve God . . . oh man, get ready. It's one moment in your chaotic teenage life where the insecurities disappear, worries fade, and questions die. For once, you know exactly who you are and why you were created. You

> Do your work with enthusiasm. Work as if you were serving the Lord.
> (Ephesians 6:7)

are in God's plan. Could there be anything better to wake up for?

There's no time like the present to get started. All over the world, people need food, friendship, clean water, acceptance, shelter, and love.

More than anything, the world needs to meet Jesus. And the best way for them to get to know him is by meeting someone like you. Someone who shows Jesus' love to them. You can share a meal, start a friendship, say a prayer. That's how the very first followers of Jesus did it. In fact, that's how Christianity first spread throughout the world. Dad describes it like this:

 MAX ||||||||||||||||||||||||||||||||||||||||||||||||||||||||||||||||||||||||||||||||||||||||||||||||||||||

There were one hundred and twenty charter members of the Jerusalem church (Acts 1:15). They were mostly lower class— fishermen, tax collectors, and a converted revolutionary or two. They had no clout with Caesar, no friends in high places. They had nothing more than this:

They were on fire to change the world.

Thanks to Luke, we know what happened with them. He recorded their stories in the book of Acts. Let's listen to it. That's right—*listen* to the book of Acts. It cracks with the sounds of God's work. Press your ear against the pages, and hear sermons echo off the temple walls. Baptismal waters splashing, just-saved souls laughing. Hear the spoon scrape the bowl as yet another hungry mouth is fed.

Listen to the doors opening and walls collapsing. Doors to all kinds of cities and countries like Antioch, Ethiopia, Corinth, and Rome. Doors into palaces, prisons, and Roman courts. And walls. The ancient prejudice between Jew and Samaritan— down! The division between Jew and Gentile—crash!

Acts announces, "God is at work!"

Is he still? we wonder. *Would God do with us what he did with his first followers?*

Heaven knows we hope so. These are devastating times. There are needs all around us. Some are big—like the 1.75 billion people who are desperately poor.[1] Some seem small—like the outcasts in your school who sit ignored in class every day. God has equipped us to make a difference, whether it's right here at home or halfway across the globe.

Ours is the richest time in history ever. We are bright, educated, and experienced. We can travel around the world in twenty-four hours or send a message in a millisecond. We have the most sophisticated research and medicines at the tips of our fingers. We have plenty of resources. Just 2 percent of the world's grain harvest would be enough, if shared, to erase the problem of hunger and malnutrition around the world.[2] There is enough food on the planet to offer every person 2,500 calories of sustenance a day.[3] We have enough food to feed the hungry.

25,000 children under age five die of preventable deaths every day.[4]

This much is clear: the storehouse is stocked. God has given us everything we need to alter the course of human suffering.

A few years back, three questions rocked my world. They came from different people in the span of a month.

Question #1: If you were a German Christian during World War II, would you have taken a stand against Hitler?

Question #2: If you had lived in the South during the civil rights conflict, would you have taken a stand against racism?

Question #3: When your grandchildren discover you lived during a day when 1.75 billion people were poor and 1 billion were hungry, how will they judge what you did to help?

I didn't mind the first two questions. I'd like to think I would have taken a stand against the murderous dictator Hitler and fought against racism. But those days are gone and those choices were not mine. But the third question has kept me awake at night. I do live today; so do you. We are given a choice . . . an opportunity to make a big difference during a difficult time. What if we did? What if we rocked the world with hope? Infiltrated all corners with God's love and life? What if we followed the example of the first Jerusalem church? This tiny group of one hundred and twenty followers expanded into a world-changing force. How did they do it? What can we learn from their priorities and passion?

Lots, if we study their stories, found in the first twelve chapters of Acts.

> Go ahead. Why not get out your Bible and read Acts 1–12 this week? Examine each event as you say this prayer: *Do it again, Jesus. Do it again.*

The message of Jesus spread because people took care of each other. They loved God and started loving the people around them. So how do you get started on your journey to change the world?

It starts with your **heart**.
You and God.
God and you.

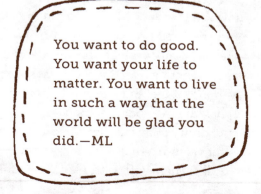

You want to do good. You want your life to matter. You want to live in such a way that the world will be glad you did. —ML

The first step on your great adventure to make a difference with God is to let him know you want a real relationship with him. Just talk to him. Tell him you're ready to take your relationship to the next level. Wherever you are in knowing God, you can go deeper. You might not be able to see him, you may not know if you have ever felt his presence, but he is right here with you. Right now, while you're reading this page. Waiting to hear from you. Waiting for you to start a conversation.

Why not talk to God now in your own words? And even if you don't see a flash of lightning or feel something right away, he'll hear you. He's rejoicing over you. You are his masterpiece.

As you get closer to God, you will start to see yourself the way he sees you. And he will show you all the things he has equipped you with to make a difference. Then, as you continue to get to know and follow him, he will take you to the people who need exactly what you can give. We know he will, because he's already making a difference with kids all over the place. Young people whose stories you'll read in the following chapters. Ordinary teens who are excited to wake up every morning, knowing they're going on grand adventures with God, changing lives in ways they never would have dreamed they could.

Just like those first Christ-followers, you have a God-designed place in history, *his story*. And making a difference will be the butterflies-in-the-stomach, worth-waking-up-for experience of a lifetime.

"I say this because I know what I am planning for you," says the LORD. "I have good plans for you, not plans to hurt you. I will give you hope and a good future."

Jeremiah 29:11

God, thank you for making us with purpose. Thank you for loving every inch of us, in spite of our messiness. Help us love you more, so that we can love others more. Give us eyes to see what you see, so that our everyday, boring routines turn into an adventure—an opportunity to serve someone, love someone, listen to someone. An opportunity to make a difference. Change us to be more like you.

In Jesus' name I pray, amen.

CHAPTER 2

PLAIN CHEESE PIZZA

You will be my witnesses—in Jerusalem, in all of
Judea, in Samaria, and in every part of the world.

Acts 1:8

A telephone rings, and a woman's voice answers.

"Joe's Pizza, may I take your order?"

"Yes, ma'am. I'd like a large pizza with spinach and Alfredo sauce, to go."

"I'm sorry. We just have plain cheese pizza."

"Oh, then I'd like a pepperoni, sausage, ham, bacon, salami, and any-other-kind-of-meat-you-can-think-of pizza."

"I'm sorry. We only serve plain cheese pizza."

"Okay, then I'd like to try your everything-but-the-kitchen-sink pizza, the one with chocolate syrup on top."

"I said, 'WE ONLY HAVE PLAIN CHEESE PIZZA!'"

"You don't have to yell. It's just that plain cheese is a little, well, boring, isn't it? Okay, fine. One cheese pizza it is."

"That will be ten dollars and sixty-nine cents. We'll see you in fifteen minutes."

Plain cheese pizza.

It may not seem very exciting, but it's tasty and filling. If you're hungry, plain cheese pizza gets the job done.

More than 3 billion pizzas a year are sold in the United States, resulting in about $37 billion in sales.

—National Association of Pizzeria Operators

The first believers in Acts were kind of like plain cheese pizza.

They didn't look like much to the rest of the world, but they sure made a difference. The world was hungry. Some were physically hungry. Many spiritually hungry. Plain cheese pizza filled them right up. The early Christians had no fancy toppings or qualifications. They were clumsy. Hardheaded and forgetful, for sure. But ambassadors? Leaders? Hope bringers?

Not quite.

Let us introduce you to some of them. The tall one in the corner—that's Peter. His biggest catch in life before meeting Jesus came with fins and gills. Strange. The guy chosen to lead the next great work of God knows more about bass and boat docks than he does about Roman culture or Egyptian leaders.

And his buddies: Andrew, James, Nathanael. Never traveled

farther than a week's walk from home. Haven't studied the ways of Asia or the culture of Greece. Their passports aren't worn; their ways aren't sophisticated.

Do they have any formal education? No. In fact, what do they have?

Humility? *Not*. They tried to push each other aside to get the best positions.

Lots of God-knowledge? *Nope*. Peter told Jesus to forget the cross.

Sensitivity? *Not hardly*. John wanted to torch the Gentiles.

Loyalty? *Epic fail*. When Jesus needed prayers, they snoozed. When Jesus was arrested, they ran. Thanks to their cowardice, Christ had more enemies than friends at his execution.

Yet look at them six weeks later, crammed into the second floor of a Jerusalem house, acting like they just won tickets to the hottest concert in town. All high fives and wide eyes. Wondering what in the world Jesus had in mind with his final charge: "You will be my witnesses in Jerusalem, and in all Judea and Samaria, and to the ends of the earth" (Acts 1:8 NIV).

You hillbillies will be my witnesses.
You uneducated and simple guys will be my witnesses.
You who once called me crazy, who shouted at me in
　　the boat and doubted me in the storm.
You temperamental fishermen and tax collectors.
You will be my witnesses.

You will head up a movement that will explode like a just-opened fire hydrant out of Jerusalem and spill into the ends of the earth: into the streets of Paris, the districts of Rome, and the ports of Athens, Shanghai, and Buenos Aires. You will be a part of something so mighty, controversial, and head spinning that two thousand years from now people are still talking about it. The question we want to know is this one:

> Does Jesus
> still use
> simple people like us
> to change the world?

We are plain cheese pizza too. Ordinary. Fans don't wave when we go by. No one serves us dinner on silver platters or hands us hundreds of dollars in allowance. Paparazzi don't follow us, and we're probably not listed in Wikipedia or famous on YouTube (at least, not yet). We, like the Jerusalem disciples, are regular people.

According to the _Guinness Book of Records_, the world's largest pizza was nearly 123 feet in diameter and took 1,100 lbs. of flour, 1,760 lbs. of cheese and 1,980 lbs. of tomato purée.

Can God still use plain cheese pizza? Absolutely.
Just ask fifteen-year-old Austin Gutwein.

AUSTIN'S STORY

Austin Gutwein just wanted to get picked for the basketball team at his school. He was nine years old, and he loved the game. Unfortunately, he wasn't that great at shooting hoops.

He didn't make the team. But he still made a difference.

He saw a video by World Vision about kids in Zambia, Africa, who were orphaned because their moms and dads had died from the disease AIDS. Austin couldn't stop thinking about what it would be like to have no parents. It made him sad to think about kids who had to do everything for themselves—

find food and cook it,

    clean up after themselves,

        put themselves to bed in an otherwise empty hut,

           keep their younger brothers and sisters alive.

Then Austin wanted to go beyond

    thinking

        about it

           and DO something about it.

Austin told his dad he wanted to help, and they called World Vision. Together, they all came up with a simple but brilliant plan. On World AIDS Day of that year (December 1, 2004), Austin would shoot a free throw in honor of every child whose parents would die that day of the awful disease.

People sponsored Austin, and he raised more than three thousand dollars.

continued »

Almost 5,500 people die every day because of Acquired Immune Deficiency Syndrome (AIDS).

—USAID.gov

**BUT IT WASN'T ENOUGH.
HE KNEW HE COULD DREAM
BIGGER
AND DO MORE.**

The next year, he got **1,000** of his friends to join him in shooting hoops and raising money. The charitable organization Hoops of Hope was born.

Austin and his Rwandan friend Samuel

THAT'S A LOT OF FRIENDS!
The average Facebook user has 130 friends.

—Facebook.com

"I honestly think that everybody does want to go out and make a difference," Austin told us.[1] "I think that there is nothing at all special about me compared to somebody else. Everybody can make a difference. They just have to be willing to try."

Because Austin was willing to try, in just five years Hoops of Hope has raised more than one million dollars. The money has been used to build schools, medical clinics, and orphanages to help kids in Africa.

ONE MILLION DOLLARS!!!

Six years later, God is still using Austin to make a difference. He has written a book to inspire others, encouraged tens of thousands of teens as a guest speaker on the national Revolve teen conference tour, and traveled to Africa to take backpacks filled with supplies to those in need.

In 2009 alone, Hoops of Hope raised:

➜ $198,000 to build dormitories for 280 children at the Jonathan Sim School in Twachiyanda, Zambia.
➜ $82,000 to build two Orphan Hope Centers in Swaziland.
➜ $120,000 to complete the funding of the Chilala clinic in Zambia.
➜ $41,000 to provide 250 bicycles and 750 mosquito nets to caregivers in Sinazongwe, Zambia.

Austin has seen firsthand how an ordinary, plain cheese

continued »

Shooting free throws at a Hoops of Hope event

pizza teen was made to make a difference, and he is having the time of his life.

"I'm just looking forward to every day," Austin says. "I have the coolest job in the world. It's definitely mind-boggling, all the things that have been done through something as simple as basketball. And the best part for me now, I think, is getting to hear how other kids every day are making a difference all over the world."

$85 will buy a water filter to give a family in Zambia, Africa, clean water for ten to twenty years. That's eighty-five free throws if sponsors donate $1 per basket. It's also less than two new Xbox games.

250 Bicycles for Caregivers

A few years ago, Austin Gutwein was just an elementary school kid who heard a sad story. He could have thought about it for a little while and forgotten about it. He could have prayed for the kids and left it at that. But he didn't.

To find out what Austin Gutwein is up to next, or to get your own group of friends together to shoot some hoops and make a difference, visit HoopsofHope.org.

➔ He told someone how much the story moved him.

➔ They came up with a plan of action.

➔ With Austin by his side, God put the plan in motion.

➔ Now needs are being met and Christ is being shared in Africa through Hoops of Hope.

Note to self: Read Austin Gutwein's book, *Take Your Best Shot*.[2]

God is taking Austin Gutwein on a great adventure, just like the one he took the disciples on when they walked this planet two thousand years ago. In fact, he prefers to pick ordinary, plain cheese pizza people so that he can do something extraordinary with them.

Before Jesus came along, the disciples were loading trucks, coaching soccer, and selling Slurpee drinks at the convenience store. There is no evidence that Jesus chose them because they were smarter or nicer than the guy next

continued »

door. The one thing they had going for them was a willingness to take a step when Jesus said, "Follow me."

Are you more canoe than cruise ship? More stand-in than movie star? Congratulations. God changes the world with teens like you.
—ML

JENNA

I grew up believing that the world could be changed. I was a missionary kid, a pastor's kid. But I didn't believe *I* could change the world until I was seventeen. That's when I went on my first-ever mission trip to Haiti.

We slept in mosquito-netted cots, lived with orphans, touched the outcasts, painted a new school . . . but there was a specific moment when God nudged my heart.

We were in a remote village in the rain forest, staying at an orphanage. That evening, after a day of playing with the kids, we clustered in the schoolhouse to sing songs to Jesus. A nine-year-old deaf orphan girl sat in my lap. She had wild hair, knobby knees, and a tattered dress. She rarely sat still. But as we were singing, she fell asleep with her head in my lap. With no electricity, we sang by candlelight. I stared into the glowing face of this peaceful orphan girl and began to cry.

My selfishness stared me in the face. The things I was living for—my senior year, prom, popularity, sports, shopping, that cute guy, vacations—all seemed meaningless.

It was just God,
a little girl,
and me.

Yet I was more content, more joyful, more peaceful than I had ever felt before.

Why?

Because I finally understood what God designed me to do—love the unloved. By rocking the little girl to sleep, I felt the satisfaction of God. It was as if he said, "I brought you here to show this little girl that I love her, that she matters to me. And there's more! I have more of my children for you to love! Will you?"

That night I answered the call God put on my heart to change the world by loving others, by telling people that they matter and that God loves them.

～～～～～～～～～～～～～～～～～～～～

What about you? Will you answer God's call? Don't be scared! God doesn't leave you hanging. He partners with you to make a difference bigger and better than you could ever do on your own. In fact, he's been loading you up with everything you need—experiences, relationships, even gifts! You just need to recognize those gifts. Since the day you were born, you've been uploading all the things you've heard, read, seen, thought, and learned. You are a walking library packed with experiences, memories, and abilities that no one else can claim. When you take a look at yourself from God's point of view, what do you see?

CALEB'S STORY

Caleb is nine years old. He plays basketball, avoids girls, and wants the kids of El Salvador to have clean drinking water. During a Sunday school class, his teacher shared the reality of life in poverty-stricken Central America. For lack of clean drinking water, children die of preventable diseases every day. Caleb was stunned and stepped into action. He took the twenty dollars he had been saving for a new video game, gave it to the cause, and asked his father to match it. He then challenged the entire staff of the children's ministry at his church to follow his example. The result? Enough money to dig two wells in El Salvador.

Okay, let's do a little self-examination. What are you good at? What are you excited about doing? What did God give you that can help you get started (friends, money, free time)? Are you a good public speaker? Do you love to make things? When people walk in your front door, do you love to make them feel at home? Do you enjoy spending time with babies and young children? Do you love to shop? Are you a good cook? Are you an athlete?

Ask three people, who know you the best, what they think your talents and strengths are. Go ahead. Why don't you put this book down and take the next fifteen minutes to ask people close to you what great stuff they see in you? Go find a family member, text your friends, or make an old-fashioned phone call to someone who knows you inside and out.

Tell them straight up, "God and I are going to change the world." Well, okay . . . so, you don't have to use those exact words, but it might help to confide in someone about all this making-a-difference stuff. They may have some good advice. They might even get excited and want to help. When your fifteen minutes are up, come back and write down the answers you got.

Ready?
Set,
GO!

You're back. Great. Now, what answers did you get? Make a list here.

1. ....

2. ....

3. ....

4. ....

5. ....

You have a lot to offer. And the world needs what you and God can do.

Memorize Psalm 139:14. It says, "I praise you because you made me in an amazing and wonderful way. What you have done is wonderful. I know this very well." This is a great verse to repeat whenever you're not feeling very special.

Are you ready to roll?

Because . . .

all over the place,

right now,

there are people who need

YOU.

➡ There are kids in your school who need a friend,
➡ families across the world who need clean water and food,
➡ someone in your neighborhood who needs a smile,
➡ a teen who needs someone to listen because her parents are splitting up,
➡ people on your street who need a helping hand,
➡ an overworked mom in your own house who needs an empty dishwasher (hint, hint).

What can you do?
Carpe diem. Seize the day.

According to the National Center for Health Statistics, the average life expectancy of an American is 77.9 years. If you take 77.9 times 365.25 days in a year, that's an average lifetime of 28,453 days. Subtract a couple thousand for the baby and toddler years, and that's still a lot of days to make a difference!

Grab your once-in-history opportunity with God and go for it with everything you've got.

That's what the disciples did. It's what the first believers in the book of Acts did. And the ripple effect of people who believed in Jesus and had their lives changed spread from Jerusalem, to nearby communities like Samaria, then to the whole world.

Think about that.
If the first believers in Jesus had kept it to themselves, you probably never would have heard of him.

It's what Austin Gutwein did, first by shooting a few baskets at his school, then by creating Hoops of Hope events across the country, and now changing lives around the world.

It's what plain cheese pizza people are doing all over the place, right now.

Now it's your turn.

Maybe you aren't sure how to talk to someone and offer help. Maybe you would feel awkward trying to comfort somebody who is crying. Maybe you have never seen anyone really, really poor or sick with disease and are afraid you might throw up! Don't worry! Sometimes all it takes is a kind "hello," a smile someone's way, or a gentle, "Can I help you in any way?" when you see someone in need. If you get turned down, that's okay too. You did the right thing to offer. It might take a chain of people to approach someone before that person accepts help. And you may be just one link in that chain. Then move on to other opportunities God shows you.

Because if you don't make a difference for Jesus, someone may miss out on what you have to give. Remember, pizza adds a lot to life, even when it's just plain cheese. In fact, a life without pizza just doesn't taste as good.

And life without Jesus means no life at all.

Pass the cheese, please.

Brothers and sisters, look at what you were when God called you. Not many of you were wise in the way the world judges wisdom. Not many of you had great influence. Not many of you came from important families. But God chose the foolish things of the world to shame the wise, and he chose the weak things of the world to shame the strong.

1 Corinthians 1:26–27

Who am I, God? On my own, I'm ordinary. But in YOU, I'm extraordinary. You have given my life a purpose. Would you show me that purpose more and more? Would you point me to people you want me to help, pray for, talk to? Use me, Father. Give me the strength and vision to make a difference. I want people to see how big you are. I want people to see that with you, ANYTHING is possible. I love you, Lord.

In Jesus' name I pray, amen.

CHAPTER 3

NO DROPPED CALLS

I loved you as the Father loved me. Now remain in my love.

Jesus, in John 15:9

Picture yourself as the contestant.

Sitting in the "hot seat" on the game show *Who Wants to Be a Millionaire?*

You've answered fourteen questions correctly, and now you're staring at the last one.

The **million-dollar** question.

Two of your lifelines are gone.

And it hits you . . .

You don't know the answer.
You have absolutely no idea.

You grab for your last lifeline, the Phone-a-Friend. Ask the host to connect you to your best friend. You're sure your friend will know how many carbon atoms there are in one molecule of glucose.

The host dials your friend's cell.

The phone rings.

It rings again. You're wiping the sweat from your brow.

Finally, your friend says, "Hello," and the host explains the reason for the call. Your friend laughs and says, "Sure, I know the answer to that one. It's—"

And the phone goes dead.

The call was dropped.

Your friend's not on the line anymore.

And you're out a million bucks.

Bummer.

There are six carbon atoms in one molecule of glucose.

In your relationship with God, what kind of connection do you have? Constant communication or a bunch of dropped calls and poor signals?

About half the world's population uses cell phones. The number of mobile subscribers world-wide reached over 2 billion by the end of 2005 and is predicted to rise to 3.96 billion by 2011.[1]

Before you can go on a world-changing adventure with Christ, you have to get connected to him. Get to know him. I mean, you don't want to spend the rest of your life on a trip with someone you don't know very well. You want to experience the best times of your life with a loving Father—One who will provide for you and protect you. One who will listen to you and love you unconditionally. That's the kind of relationship Jesus wants to have with you.

You and him . . .
Meeting people, going places, changing things . . .
Sharing it all together.

 JENNA

Everything was packed.

Swimsuit? Check. Shorts? Check. Sunscreen? Check. T-shirts? Check. And that was it. All I needed. After all, I was going on vacation to the beach. What else does anyone need?! Okay, maybe some floss. But who needs shampoo or deodorant? I practically live in the water, so there is no dry moment to smell any b.o, or see oily hair. (You are probably gagging a little bit right now.) To be honest, I packed shampoo and deodorant. But to be even more honest, I hate showering, dressing up, and wearing make-up. That's why I love beach life.

So I had everything I needed, all packed up and ready to go.

We got to the airport. I had my plane ticket, my snacks, my books. I thought I was all set for vacation—until Dad asked for everyone's ID.

I took out my wallet confidently, sifted through the cards. Credit card, gift card, gas card . . . but no driver's license, no school ID! My heart sank. I thought I was ready. I thought I had everything. But my ticket to adventure was gone.

Could I have downloaded ocean sounds on iTunes, sat at the edge of the neighborhood pool on my towel as I sipped a Coke, and pretended I was at the beach? Sure. But it wouldn't have been the same. Not nearly as beautiful or breathtaking. No gazing at endless water and clear, blue sky. Just the five-foot-deep pool and city haze.

Jesus is the ticket to adventure. He brings fulfillment, joy, and the supernatural power to change hearts when we remember to include him in our quest to make a difference. When we don't drop our connection.

Can we serve without God? Sure.

But the experience isn't nearly as beautiful or breathtaking.

Thankfully, I didn't have to hang out at the neighborhood pool. A friend brought my ID to the airport just in time for takeoff. Thankfully, we don't have to pack anything to go on an adventure. All we need is Jesus. Just talk to him, and he'll always be there, ready to go.

~~~~~~~~~~~~~~~~~~~~~~~~~~~~~~~~~~~~~

When you remember to take God everywhere you go, you will change—in a good way. He will help you be kinder to classmates who bug you. Obedient to the parents who get on your case. Enthusiastic about giving up your time or your money to help.

God's love softens your heart.
Changes your attitude.
Makes you a new—and—improved version of your old self.

He's the real "lifeline."

God is your 24/7 "Phone-a-Friend." In Jeremiah 33:3, God says, "Call to Me, and I will answer you, and show you great and mighty things, which you do not know" (NKJV).

 This is what a real relationship with Jesus is like:

TOP 10 REASONS WHY JESUS IS AWESOME TO HANG OUT WITH

1. He always says nice things about you.
2. He never fights with you or gets so mad he refuses to speak to you.
3. He is a true love who will never break up with you or break your heart.
4. He gives you more than anyone ever has.
5. He listens to every word you say and understands everything you feel.
6. He can't wait to go places and do stuff with you.
7. He has invitations to the most exciting places—and takes you with him.
8. He sees you as perfect just the way you are. He never fakes it or just tells you what you want to hear. To him, you are absolutely awesome.
9. He listens when you admit every wrong thing you've ever done, and you never have to feel guilty or ashamed.
10. He forgives you completely and never brings up any of your mistakes again!

Scientific studies show that forgiveness helps hearts stay healthy, leads to lower blood pressure, and relieves stress.

—Mayoclinic.com

Jesus was born into this world. He was cut down, bruised, and beaten on the threshing floor of Calvary. He passed through the fire of God's wrath, for our sake. He "suffered because of others' sins, the Righteous One for the unrighteous ones. He went through it all—was put to death and then made alive— to bring us to God" (1 Peter 3:18 MSG).

Have you received God's forgiveness? —ML

Isn't that the kind of relationship with God you'd like to have all the time? Well, when you build a connection with Jesus, you do! Then you can introduce him to everyone you know. Everyone you meet along the way. Because when you have a Father who makes you feel great and makes life fun and exciting, don't you want others to have that too? When you love God, you can overflow his amazing love everywhere you go. His kind of love is contagious. It makes a difference.

First John 4:8 breaks it down for us like this: "Whoever does not love does not know God, because God is love."

Did you catch that last part? God *is* love. In math word problems, when you see the word "is," you know (at least, you're supposed to know) it means "equals."

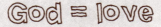

Know God, and you will experience real love. Then you can pass it on.

Growing up in a Christian home, faith came easily to me at first. I believed in God and knew he loved me, but I hadn't spent time getting to know this love *personally*. Because I didn't know God in relationship, I peaked out on my faith. I had no ties. I hung out with people who didn't get into the God thing, and I let their lifestyles influence me. I got caught in the gossip web and hung up on boys. God wasn't a priority. In fact, I went through a phase where I doubted his existence altogether. And that's when I hit my darkest point.

I was empty, without hope. I knew I wanted something more. I broke down and told God that I needed him, and he revealed himself to me in a new way. This new way was personal. It wasn't my parents' faith; it was my own, because I spent time *getting to know* the true, intimate God.

He died for *me*. Even when I wanted nothing to do with him, failed him, disowned him, he never disowned me. No one on earth could EVER love me as completely, deeply, and faithfully as Jesus Christ. Jesus lived a perfect life, yet died a sinner's death (the death that I deserved). Then he defeated death, so that I could live with him forever.

The more I spent time with God, the more I told others about him. I couldn't help it! When you know the drenching, quenching love of God, you slosh it onto others. Why keep such good news to yourself?

~~~~~~~~~~~~~~~~~~~~~~~~~~~~~~~~~~~~~~

Now it's time to ask again: How's your connection with God? Is Jesus the BIG story in your life? When did you become part of his story?

Here's some space for you to write down your thoughts about what your relationship with God is like right now. What would you like it to be?

....

....

....

....

....

....

If you don't remember ever asking Christ to be part of your life, will you do it now? He wants a relationship with you, just like you are. You don't have to get your act together or be a better person first.

Just talk to him.

Ask him to forgive you for the things you've done wrong. He will.

You could say something like this:

> *God, I need you.*
>
> *I realize that my heart is messed up. I have made so many mistakes. I have turned to others, even myself, to find purpose and happiness. Please forgive me for not turning to you, the Giver of life.*
>
> *I believe that Jesus Christ is the Son of God and that he lived on this earth, died on the cross, and rose again, so that I could be in a relationship with him and go to heaven. Please take over my life. I want to give it to you. I want to put my trust in you.*
>
> *Take over my heart.*
>
> *Change it.*
>
> *Help me through this new relationship with you. Thank you for loving me so much. Help me love you more.*
>
> *Amen.*

God loved the world so much that he gave his one and only Son so that whoever believes in him may not be lost, but have eternal life.

(John 3:16)

Change your hearts and lives and be baptized, each one of you, in the name of Jesus Christ for the forgiveness of your sins. And you will receive the gift of the Holy Spirit.
(Acts 2:38)

God does not give us what we deserve. He has drenched his world in grace. It has no end. It knows no limits. It empowers this life and enables us to live the next. God offers second chances, like a soup kitchen offers meals to everyone who asks. And that includes you.—ML

JESSICA'S STORY

Jessica Woolbright doesn't run a charity or raise millions of dollars. But she touches a lot of lives around her, volunteering at a local crisis pregnancy center, helping her mom with her younger brothers and sisters, and looking for needs she and Jesus can meet together.

Jessica grew up in a big Christian family and asked Jesus into her heart when she was five. But it's only been in the last few years that she's gotten really close to God. See, when Jessica was fourteen, her dad died suddenly. He was only thirty-nine years old. That's when Jessica's relationship with Jesus began to change.

"At first, I was just really mad. I hurt so much, even being around my friends didn't really help," Jessica told us.[2] "I stayed angry for a long time. I just didn't care. How could God let my Dad die?"

After months of withdrawing from friends and family, Jessica started reading her Bible again and praying. At first, she just did it so she could answer yes when her mom asked her if she had done her quiet time. Then Jessica began to notice that she felt different when she made talking to God part of her daily routine.

"Sometimes, the peace and calm I felt even in the midst of the pain were almost overwhelming," Jessica says. "I knew he was there, helping me through it."

As Jessica's connection with God grew stronger, the real adventure began. She sensed God leading her to Washington, D.C., where she worked in the U.S. House of Representatives as a congressional page. She found lots of opportunities to stand up for what she believed, encouraging girls in the program to make good relationship choices and to respect

Jessica Woolbright in Washington, D.C.

continued »

and protect their hearts and bodies. She and God have gone other places, too, such as to Mexico to help build a church and to China to visit and play with orphaned children with medical needs.

Jessica with an orphan in China

Today, Jessica makes a difference at her local community college, volunteering for student government activities and talking openly about her faith to friends. She is working toward a degree in social work so that she can help children.

"When I'm close to God, I'm not so focused on myself," Jessica says. "I don't worry about my life as much. I can definitely tell the difference when I don't make the effort. So I try to remember that and stay as close to him as I can. Then I feel his love more, and it's a lot easier to share him with others."

It's hard to feel like Jesus is real sometimes if you have never really needed anything. If your life is comfortable, what needs to be saved? To experience God in a way you never have before, go see real need. Take a short-term missions trip to help others in very poverty-stricken places. When you see people who love God because he is all they have, your faith will be strengthened as you help them. Two Christian missions organizations that have taken teens around the world are Teen Mania's Global Expeditions and Teen Missions International. Visit globalexpeditions.com or teenmissions.org.

Like Jessica discovered, once you have a real relationship with Jesus, you can introduce him to others. After all, if we don't, who will?

Governments can give people food and other assistance, but they don't feed people's souls. Charities can give a bed, a meal, and good advice. But Christ-followers can give much more. Not just help for this life, but hope for the next. —ML

No broken connections. A relationship with God is a lifeline that will never break. Unlike cell phones, your signal with God can always be strong. A call to God will never be dropped. And that's worth a whole lot more than a million dollars. So . . .

Can you hear him?
Can you hear him now?

God was in Christ, making peace between the world and himself. In Christ, God did not hold the world guilty of its sins. And he gave us this message of peace. So we have been sent to speak for Christ. It is as if God is calling to you through us. We speak for Christ when we beg you to be at peace with God. Christ had no sin, but God made him become sin so that in Christ we could become right with God.

2 Corinthians 5:19–21

God, give me boldness to share my faith with my friends. Give me the desire to serve. You promise that when we draw near to you, you will draw near to us (James 4:8). May I remember to draw near to you in every circumstance, so that your love can overflow into every corner of my life. Thank you for being a close God. Thank you for hearing me when I pray. I love you.

In Jesus' name I pray, amen.

CHAPTER 4

HIDDEN TREASURE

> But while Peter was in prison, the church prayed very earnestly for him.
>
> Acts 12:5 NLT

Can you think of two words that send a thrill down the spines of almost everyone who hears them?

We can.

Want to know what they are?

Okay, here you go.

Hidden treasure.

That little phrase sent your imagination soaring, didn't it? Just two little words, but they are packed with possibilities.

Gold coins.

Jewels.

Maybe even **pirate booty**.

Guess what?

When you deepen your relationship with God, you have your own personal stash of hidden treasure. Really, you do. It's brighter than any hip-hop star's bling. It's just waiting for you to uncover it.

It's called *prayer*.
It's powerful.
It's priceless.
And it's just what this world needs.

On treasure maps, an X often marks the spot where hidden treasure can be found. X is also the symbol for the Greek letter "Chi," which is often used as an abbreviation for Christ. X marks the spot where your hidden treasure can be found!

MAX

The Bible is full of examples of the power that real, heartfelt, persistent prayer holds. Let's go back to ancient Israel, back to visit the first church in Acts.

Peter was in prison, and King Herod was planning to execute him. This was a huge problem for the first believers. It was as big as a Goliath towering over the humble community. They had no way to help him: no clout, no political chips to cash. They had nothing but fear-drenched questions. "Who's next? First James, then Peter. Is Herod going to get rid of all the church leadership?"

Today, Christ-followers in the church still face Goliaths. World hunger. Stingy Christians. Corrupt officials. Pea-brained and hard-hearted dictators.

Peter in prison is just the first of a long list of challenges too big for the church. So our Jerusalem ancestors left us a strategy. When the problem is bigger than we are—we pray! "But while Peter was in prison, the church prayed very earnestly for him" (Acts 12:5 NLT).

They didn't picket the prison, petition the government, protest the arrest, or prepare for Peter's funeral.

They prayed.

They prayed as if prayer was their only hope, because it was.

They prayed "very earnestly for him."

Prayer helps you change the world from your knees up. God waits for you to have a conversation with him. About your day. About your friends. About your hopes, dreams, and even your current crush.

> He wants to hear your problems,
>   and he wants to whisper his plans to you.
> That's right.
> When you take time to talk to him,
>   and when you stay still enough to listen,
>   pretty soon you will know when God is speaking
>   to your heart.

You probably won't hear a voice out loud, but you will start to recognize when God is giving you peace, joy, love, and understanding.

Isn't it amazing that the God who created the whole

universe wants you to ask him for everything you need? You're so important to him that he is waiting eagerly to talk to you—all the time. Think about that. God is waiting to chat with you!

Okay, so sometimes praying can feel like talking to the air, especially if we have fallen into the habit of reciting childhood rhymes before bedtime and quickly offering a well-rehearsed line or two before we eat.

What would happen if we really prayed?

If talking to God was something we did as naturally and as often as breathing, how would our lives—and the world around us—be different?

> Pray in the Spirit at all times with all kinds of prayers, asking for everything you need. To do this you must always be ready and never give up. Always pray for all God's people.
> (Ephesians 6:18)

Studies conducted by Harvard, Duke, and Yale universities have shown that prayer has healing power. For example, hospitalized people who don't attend church have an average stay of three times longer than people who attend regularly.

God has wired his world for power, but he calls on us to flip the switch.

And the Jerusalem church did just that.

The church prayed very earnestly for Peter. —ML

Our passionate prayers move the heart of God. Prayer impacts the flow of history.

Emily Chapman Richards knows the power that prayer holds. Her prayers for a little sister took her on an adventure all over the world.

EMILY'S STORY

When Emily Chapman was eleven years old, she went on a mission trip to Haiti and saw the needs of orphaned children with her own eyes. It changed her life.

"Prior to my trip to Haiti, I had never traveled outside of the United States of America," Emily told us.[1] "My eyes were opened to the bitter realities poverty presents as I walked the streets of Haiti and talked with the people. I met kids my own age who didn't have homes to go home to, children who were

continued »

Emily Chapman Richards and her three sisters, who were adopted from China

wondering how they would make it to the next meal and to the next day."

About 9 million people live in Haiti, the poorest country in North America, South America, or their associated islands. The capital city is Port-Au-Prince. On January 12, 2010, Port-Au-Prince was devastated by an earthquake that registered 7.0 on the Richter scale. It killed an estimated 150,000 people and left as many as 30,000 children without parents.

Emily continued, "I returned home to America with the eyes of my heart wide open and aware of God's work worldwide. I honestly believe God burdened my heart for orphans during my trip to Haiti, and it was in praying and seeking God that I began to understand that Christ through me could make a positive difference in the world."

Once home, Emily came up with the idea that her family could adopt a little sister. Emily had two younger brothers, and her family had the resources to give a child a home.

"After my trip to Haiti, I simply began asking God how I was to respond to the great need I witnessed," Emily says. "I was only eleven years old. What could I do for the world's 130 million-plus orphans?"

Her parents weren't as excited as Emily about her idea. Still, she persisted. She used her Christmas money to buy a book on international adoption and read it to her mom when they rode in the car. She left notes about it on her parents' pillows and even told them they weren't following God's will, because the Bible says to care for orphans! She was so convinced that her family was supposed to adopt and that her parents weren't getting the message that she made an appointment to talk to her pastor. She asked him what she should do to make her parents adopt. He encouraged her to seek what God wanted for her family, not just what she wanted, and to continue praying about it. So she did. She prayed and prayed.

Her parents slowly got the message that maybe adoption should be part of their family story. Today, the family has adopted three daughters from China. Plus, they started an organization called Show Hope, which gives grants (free money!) to help other families adopt. Show Hope also sponsors orphans, helps churches start adoption ministries, and has even built an orphanage in China for kids with special needs called Maria's Big House of Hope.

continued »

Maria's Big House of Hope in Luoyang, China

Because of an eleven-year-old's faithful, not-giving-up prayers, not only did she get

ONE little sister;

she got THREE.

Because of her faithful, not-giving-up prayers, now

HUNDREDS

of children with special needs have a warm, safe place to live,

HUNDREDS

of churches are learning how to help families in their communities adopt,

and

THOUSANDS

of children are finding families.

"Never underestimate the power of prayer!" Emily says. "While it's important to be actively involved in outreach opportunities and ministry events, we must remember that anything and everything we do is only possible because of Christ living in and through us. The statistics are paralyzing, and we cannot do the work on our own; therefore, it is important to cry out to God for his help and guidance in regards to helping the hurting."

Today, Emily is married and studying at a Bible college in Northern Ireland. She works for Show Hope and plans to adopt children of her own someday. And she still prays. She knows it works! It's a priceless treasure.

You can change the life of a child by sponsoring an orphan, praying for orphans living at Maria's Big House of Hope, collecting change for Show Hope, starting an orphan ministry at your church, or even buying a Show Hope T-shirt. Get great ideas at ShowHope.org.

Write down James 5:16 and tape it to your mirror, your locker, or somewhere you will see it a lot. Memorize it!

Confess your sins to each other and pray for each other so God can heal you. When a believing person prays, great things happen. (James 5:16)

Did those prayers for Peter make a difference to the first church in Jerusalem too? You bet they did. The church cried out to their loving Father, and he responded.

> The night before Peter was to be placed on trial, he was asleep, fastened with two chains between two soldiers. Others stood guard at the prison gate. Suddenly, there was a bright light in the cell, and an angel of the Lord stood before Peter. The angel struck him on the side to awaken him and said, "Quick! Get up!" And the chains fell off his wrists. Then the angel told him, "Get dressed and put on your sandals." And he did. "Now put on your coat and follow me," the angel ordered. (Acts 12:6–8 NLT)

Stunned, Peter walks to Mary's house. She, at that very hour, is hosting a prayer meeting on his behalf. His friends pack the place. Peter surely smiles as he hears their prayers. He knocks on the door. The servant answers and, instead of opening it, races back to the prayer circle and announces:

> "Peter is standing at the door!"
> "You're out of your mind!" they said. When she insisted, they decided, "It must be his angel." (vv. 14–15 NLT)

Even the early followers struggled to believe God would hear them. Even when the answer knocked on the door, they hesitated.

We still do. Most of us struggle with prayer. We forget to pray, and when we remember, we hurry through prayers. Our minds drift; our thoughts scatter like homework pages in the wind. Why is this? Prayer requires very little effort. You don't have to pray in a particular place. You don't have to wear special clothes. You don't have to be someone important for God to hear you. Yet you'd think we were wrestling a greased pig.

Speaking of pigs, Satan also seeks to interrupt our prayers. The devil witnessed the angel in Peter's cell and the revival in Jerusalem. He knows what happens when we pray. "Our weapons have power from God that can destroy the enemy's strong places" (2 Corinthians 10:4).

Satan does not stutter or stumble when you walk through church doors or attend youth group. Demons aren't flustered when you read this book. But the walls of hell shake when one teen with an honest heart and faithful confession says, "Oh, God, you are so awesome."

Satan keeps you and me from prayer. He tries to position himself between us and God. But he scampers like a spooked dog when we move forward. So let's do it.

Here's what happens to our connection with God when we pray:

Humble yourselves before God. Resist the devil, and he will flee from you. Come close to God, and God will come close to you. (James 4:7–8 NLT)

The LORD is close to everyone who prays to him, to all who truly pray to him. (Psalm 145:18)

Let us, then, feel very sure that we can come before God's throne where there is grace. There we can receive mercy and grace to help us when we need it. (Hebrews 4:16)

You can pray with your eyes closed or open. You can bow your head or keep your head up. You can sing prayers, write prayers, or recite prayers from prayer guides or prayer books (that you can often get at church).

JENNA

It took me awhile to learn that prayer was not genie-in-a-bottle magic. My prayers used to be brief and typically sounded like this: "God, PLEASE give me an A on this algebra test!" or "God, please help that guy to notice me." Now, I'm not saying that praying for yourself is bad, but I *am* saying to check your motives. Are you praying so that your wishes will be granted or that God's will be done?

Prayer takes practice. It's not just about talking; it's about listening. When there is a two-way conversation taking place, between God and us, we figure out that sometimes we are praying for the wrong thing.

My friend Mel struggles a lot with her parents, especially her mom. It's a constant war zone at home. If you got to meet her, I bet she would tell you that a couple of years ago her prayers sounded like this, "God, please just show my mom that she's wrong, I'm right, and please get her off my back!" But the more she began to get into the Bible, spend time with God, and listen, the more she realized that her prayers stemmed from a hardened heart. God showed her that her prayers should be for her own heart first, then for her mom's heart. And it worked! He answered Mel's request for peace at home, but in a totally different way. Now, her prayers are more in step with God.

Prayer not only changes the lives of others, it also changes us. It draws us deeper in tune with God's desires so that we want what he wants. And what *he* wants is always the best in the end.

Prayer is our foundation for making a difference. Trying to change the world without prayer is like trying to use a new iPod without charging the battery. You have to connect to the power source before you can start rockin'.

So:

Let's pray, *first*.

Helping a friend through social drama? Pray first. Standing up to a bully? Talk to God about it. Traveling to help the hungry? Be sure to bathe your mission in prayer. Weary with a world full of racism and division? So is God. And he would love to talk to you about it.

Grab a notebook or journal and start writing down the things you are praying for. Put the date down each time you write. Make a list of your prayer requests and include the answers to prayers as you get them. After a month, go back to the first page and thank God for the difference prayer makes!

Let's pray, *most*.

Did God call us to preach all the time? Or teach all the time? Or have classes or basketball practices all the time? Or sing all the time? No, but he did call us to pray all the time. "Pray without ceasing" (1 Thessalonians 5:17 NKJV).

The next time you will be at home all day, try a "prayer experiment": set a timer and pray every hour. See how close you feel to God after a full day of conversation!

Did Jesus declare: My house shall be called a house of study? Fellowship? Music? A house of activities? No, but he did say, "My house will be called a house of prayer" (Mark 11:17 NIV).

No other spiritual activity is guaranteed such results. "When two of you get together on anything at all on earth and make a prayer of it, my Father in heaven goes into action" (Matthew 18:19 MSG).

If you want to make a difference, talk to God.

When have you felt the closest to God in prayer?

....

....

....

What answers to prayer have you personally experienced?

....

....

....

....

....

....

....

Even Jesus, the Son of God and fully God himself, prayed.
Check out these verses:

→ Jesus woke up early to pray (see Mark 1:35).

→ Jesus dismissed people to pray (see Matthew 14:23).

→ Jesus went up a mountain to pray (see Luke 9:28).

→ Jesus taught us to pray (see Matthew 6:9–13).

→ Jesus cleansed the temple so others could pray
   (see Matthew 21:12–13).

→ Jesus stepped into a garden to pray (see Luke 22:39–46).

Let's follow Jesus' example and uncover the hidden treasure of prayer.

Let's pray earnestly, like the early church prayed for Peter. Because God is moved by the humble, prayerful heart.

It's powerful.
It's priceless.
It's your hidden treasure.

Continue praying, keeping alert, and always thanking God.

Colossians 4:2

Who am I, that I would have the privilege of talking to the God of the universe?! Who am I, that I would have the honor of holding the Word of God in my hands? But God, you know my heart. I'm not always excited to talk to you, and sometimes the Bible seems boring. Please change my heart and give me a greater desire to talk to you. Listen to you. Share life with you. Put on my heart the names of people you want me to pray for. I ask that before I do ANYTHING, you remind me to get on my knees. That's where the power is. It's where my treasure is. I love you.

In Jesus' name I pray, amen.

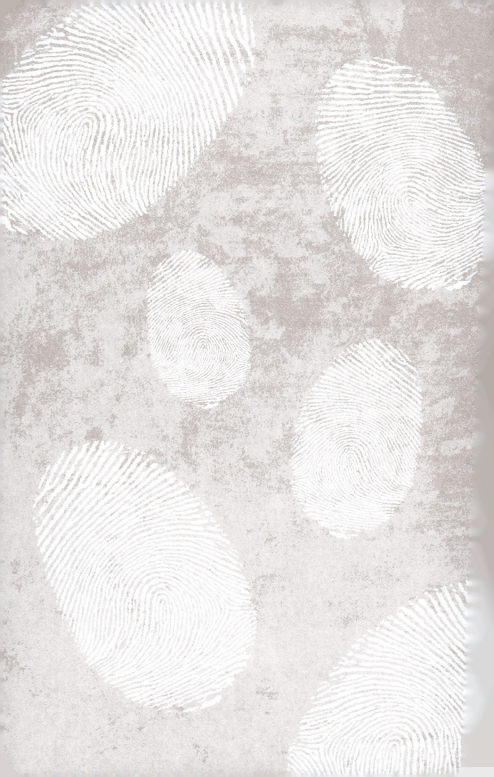

PART 2

YOU WERE MADE TO REACH OUT TO OTHERS

Over three billion people in the world each live on less than $2.50 a day. That's less than three iTunes downloads.

UNPLUG NOW!

God has big plans for me! (Jeremiah 29:11)

HELP SOMEONE!!

How does God see me?

WITH GOD'S HELP, I WILL MAKE A DIFFERENCE TODAY.

CHAPTER 5

UNPLUG AND TUNE IN

"He helped those who were poor and needy, so everything went well for him. That is what it means to know God," says the LORD.

Jeremiah 22:16

 JENNA

Is it just me, or have you also noticed that this world is plugged—plugged in, plugged up—just plain *plugged* with headphones? Every time I grocery shop, travel, jog, or just walk down the street, it seems as if every other person has some type of Bluetooth, MP3 player, or headphones shoved in his or her ears. Sure, I love a good iPod jam session. I'm up for watching an entertaining movie on the plane. But have we gone a little overboard? A little too headphone-happy?

Maybe it's time for us to take 'em out.

Pull those plugs.

Not completely. I'm not grounding you. (I really sound

like your parents right now, don't I?) I just think we all need a little vacation from headphones.

And this vacation will look and SOUND different than a plugged-up life.

Let me prepare you for some of the new sounds and sights you may encounter when you go on a headphone break. When you get unplugged.

You might get to listen to Sunny. Sunny is forty-five years old but looks like she's seventy. She lives under the bridge downtown. She can't remember the last time she was sober, but as soon as she starts telling the tales about where she has lived, slept, and visited, she lures you in. What a storyteller she is! And what a laugh she has!

You may notice Molly. Molly is the single mom in front of you at the Wal-Mart checkout line. She thought she had saved up enough money to buy her son a couple of birthday presents, but as the cashier announces the total, you watch her freeze and whisper under her breath, "Oh, no. I don't have that kind of money." She pretends to search for her wallet, then makes up a socially acceptable excuse. "I'm sorry. I must have left my wallet in the car," Molly mumbles.

With your ears uncovered, you might hear sad and empty tones you hadn't noticed before in a friend's voice when you hang out on the weekend. It could lead to a conversation about parents who have been fighting a lot. Be forewarned: you may hear and feel the needs of those around you.

Doesn't sound like a vacation, does it? Headphones protect us from other people's pain. No wonder the world is plugged. But if we want to make a difference in this world, we can't afford to be.

We've deepened our relationship with Christ. Uncovered

the hidden treasure of prayer. And now we've pulled our plugs. Only to want to shove them right back in again.

Because the idea of making a difference sounded great. Exciting, even.

The reality of making a difference? Maybe not so much. The sounds of despair, hurt, and need aren't pretty. They're not a great jam session, more like some really loud, discordant static. Noise that we can't tune out or turn off once our hearts are connected to Christ.

What if making a difference means your heart will ache because of the poverty you see and the terrible stories you'll hear? What if making a difference means you have to become friends with people you don't really like? What if making a difference means giving up things you want for yourself?

How can you get your heart ready to make a difference?

Even when you are trying to stay connected to God 24/7 and reach out to others with his love, Satan tries to distract you. It's not that he always tries to get you to commit some terrible, awful sin. Just getting your mind off of God and focused on PlayStation3, social drama among your friends, or even a good football game will do. Now, we're not saying that you shouldn't ever have fun. But if the devil can distract you on a regular basis, God gets shoved to the back shelf. Your heart gets "plugged." When you continually let go of your focus on God, the needs of others may bounce right off you.

MAX ||||||||||||||||||||||||||||||||||||||||||||||||||||||||||||||||||||||||||||||

Most of us have learned to insulate ourselves against the hurt of the hurting. Haven't we? *Mustn't* we? After all, what can we do about the famine in Sudan, the people who don't have any jobs, classmates being bullied? We want to help. But the world's problems are huge (Did you say one billion are poor?), difficult (When is helping actually hurting?), and intense (I have enough problems of my own.).

That's true. We do have our own issues.

Some of those issues may be sputtering self-esteem that says you can't do anything, too-small allowances that won't pay for much, loads of homework that drain you, entertainment that eats up your time, and stubborn hearts that don't want to feel the hurt. How can you change the world when you can't even change your bad habits? You don't have what it takes to solve the world's problems. Best to give up or turn away, right? But you can't.

The band MercyMe has created a fictional character called The Generous Mr. Lovewell to encourage Christ-followers to perform random acts of generosity toward people they don't know. Mr. Lovewell can be followed on Twitter. "Tweets" suggest things like "Pay for a stranger's lunch today."

Visit MrLovewell.com.

JENNA

Once you welcome God into your heart, it gets tough to stay plugged. His heart for the lonely, ache for the oppressed, and sadness for the poor begin to infect you (in a good way). The more we draw near him, the more we start to look, think, and act like him. The headphones stay in our rooms while our hearts reach out to the world around us.

Sure, the sounds of pain aren't as pleasant as your favorite music mix, but when you start this adventure with God, he gives you his Spirit to help you out. And pretty soon the sounds are less disturbing and more exciting—a chance to help, a chance to change the world! And in the process of helping others, you find out that you are the one who gets the blessing, because you become part of something wonderful.

If you could have anything from God that would help you help others, what would it be (for example: more money to give, courage to speak up, a great singing voice)? Why?

....

....

....

....

....

....

About 63.4 million Americans, or 26.8 percent of the population, volunteered through or for an organization at least once between September 2008 and September 2009. That number was up from 26.4 percent the year before.

—U.S. Bureau of Labor Statistics

Look what happened to the Jerusalem church when God "unplugged" them on the Day of Pentecost.

MAX ||||||||||||||||||||||||||||||||||||||||||||||||||||||||||||||||||||||||||||||||||||||||||||||||||||||||||||||||||||||

Pentecost was the busiest day of the year in Jerusalem—one of three feast days that all Jewish men, at some point in their lifetimes, were required to appear in the city. They traveled from Europe, Asia, and Africa. It's difficult to know the population of ancient cities, but some suggest that during this season Jerusalem swelled to ten times the usual population—from a hundred thousand to a million inhabitants.[1]

Her narrow streets ran thick with people of all shades of skin, from Ethiopian ebony to Roman olive. A dozen dialects bounced off the stone walls, and the temple treasury overflowed with every coin and currency.

Then there were the locals. The butcher and his meat. The wool comber and his loom. The shoemaker, hammering sandals. The tailor, plying his needle. White-robed priests and unsightly beggars. Every element of humanity crammed within the three hundred acres of the City of David.

And somewhere in their midst, Jesus' followers were

gathered in prayer. "When the Day of Pentecost had fully come, they were all with one accord in one place" (Acts 2:1 NKJV). This is the earliest appearance of the church. Consider where God placed his people. Not isolated in a desert. Not separated from society, but smack-dab in the center of it, in the heart of one of the largest cities at its busiest time.

And then, once he had them where he needed them . . .

> And suddenly there came a sound from heaven, as of a rush-ing mighty wind, and it filled the whole house where they were sitting. Then there appeared to them divided tongues, as of fire, and one sat upon each of them. And they were all filled with the Holy Spirit and began to speak with other tongues, as the Spirit gave them utterance. (vv. 2–4 NKJV)

The Holy Spirit came upon them *suddenly*—roaring like a tornado through Jerusalem. "[The sound] filled the whole house" (v. 2) and spilled into the streets. The whistling, rush-ing, blowing sound of a wind.

The Spirit came, first as wind, then appeared as individual tongues of fire, "and one sat upon each of them" (v. 3). This wasn't one torch over the entire room but individual flames hovering above each person.

And then the most unexpected thing happened.

> [They] began to speak with other tongues, as the Spirit gave them utterance. And there were dwelling in Jerusalem Jews, devout men, from every nation under heaven. And when this sound occurred, the multitude came together, and were confused, because everyone heard them speak in his own lan-guage. Then they were all amazed and marveled, saying to one another, "Look, are not all these who speak Galileans?

And how is it that we hear each in our own language in which we were born? Parthians and Medes and Elamites, those dwelling in Mesopotamia, Judea and Cappadocia, Pontus and Asia, Phrygia and Pamphylia, Egypt and the parts of Libya adjoining Cyrene, visitors from Rome, both Jews and proselytes, Cretans and Arabs—we hear them speaking in our own tongues the wonderful works of God." So they were all amazed and perplexed, saying to one another, "Whatever could this mean?" (vv. 4–12 NKJV)

Picture such a thing. Imagine a theme park on a blazing hot day during summer vacation. The ride lines are packed with families from all over the world, tourists from Spain, the Ukraine, Colombia, Korea, and Idaho. Early one morning as the mobs fill the park, the sound of a wind shakes the attractions. The roar is so loud that people stop dead in their tracks. Silence falls, only to be interrupted suddenly by the voices of a group gathered next to the biggest roller coaster. One hundred and twenty people speak, each one with a flame over their heads, explaining God's goodness in a different language. Vacationing families hear their native tongues. José, from Spain, hears about God's mercy in Spanish. Mako, from Japan, hears a message in Japanese. The group from the Philippines discerns Tagalog. They hear different languages but one message: the wonders of God.

Pretty mind-blowing.

There are approximately 6,809 spoken languages in the world today.

—Ethnologue.com

MAX

What could this mean?

At least this much: God loves the nations. He loves Iraqis. Somalians. Israelis. New Zealanders. Hondurans. He has a white-hot passion to harvest his children from every jungle, neighborhood, village, and slum. His vision for the end of history includes "people for God from *every* tribe, language, people, and nation" (Revelation 5:9, emphasis added).

God loves subcultures: the gypsies of Turkey, the hippies of California, the cowboys of West Texas, and students in Tennessee. He has a heart for bikers and hikers, tree huggers and bookworms. Single moms. Businessmen. And teens. He loves all people groups, and he works through us to be his voice. He picks common Galileans, Nebraskans, Texans, Floridians, Brazilians, and Koreans to speak the languages of the peoples of the world. He teaches us how to understand people from distant lands. God equips his followers to cross cultures and touch hearts.

Who is the person in your life who drives you the most crazy? Your sister? Your dad? A teacher you think is out to get you? What could change if you prayed for that person—really, truly prayed every day? Multiple times a day? That person may not change a bit. Their behavior may still be obnoxious. But we guarantee you this: if you are faithful, God will help you see your pain-in-the-neck person in a whole new way.

You are his follower, and just like the first believers on the Day of Pentecost, he has equipped you to change your world.

You may not stand next to a roller coaster speaking Swahili, but you are called to do something big for his kingdom.

> If you want to give something to people who stand on the side of the road with signs that say "Hungry," consider working with a volunteer group that helps street people. You could pack some snack bags with items like juice boxes or water bottles, crackers, nuts, and cereal bars or granola. Maybe even donate restaurant gift cards to add to the bags.

 JENNA

Let's daydream for a second. Think about the last time you did something well, and it came naturally to you. Was it programming the remote control, cleaning the kitchen, writing a poem for English class, scoring the most points at your homecoming game?

Now pair that up with people. How can you use that gift that comes so naturally? How can you use what you do so well to help someone else?

Could you pair the two together?

Take your gift and gift someone else.

Pull your plugs so you can do your part.

MAX

Who do you feel the most comfortable helping? Other teens? Outcasts? The elderly? You may be tongue-tied around adults but find it easy to talk to young children. This is how God designed you. "God has given us different gifts for doing certain things well" (Romans 12:6 NLT).

If you want to discover some of the gifts God planted in you, get to know yourself better. There are fun quizzes online and in many books that can help you understand what kind of personality you have, how your brain is wired, what kinds of talents you have, and more. To discover your personality type, love languages, spiritual gifts, and learning styles visit YLCF.org. A good book that contains these quizzes is *Wired by God* by Joe White and Larry K. Weeden.[2]

Who do you feel the most compassion for? God hasn't wired us to want to help everyone equally. "The LORD looks from heaven; He sees all the sons of men. . . . *He fashions their hearts individually*" (Psalm 33:13, 15, NKJV, emphasis added). When does your heart break and your pulse race? When you spot the homeless? When you see the projects in your city? When you see the victims of bullying? When you meet a really sick child?

If you need to raise money for a great cause, consider grabbing some friends and forming a babysitting co-op. Create a schedule where you can babysit in pairs and rotate weekend nights during the month so that everyone in the co-op babysits once or twice a month. Another great way to make a difference is for your babysitting co-op to give your services free to struggling families or single parents.

Leeland Mooring was just a skinny, red-haired, freckle-faced eleven-year-old when he discovered that music is the language God put inside him to change the lives of the people he meets.

LEELAND'S STORY

"I grew up in church and my parents were in music ministry, but I was a typical kid," Leeland told us.[3] "I loved being wild, running around. Then when I was eleven, I really felt the overwhelming presence and the love of God for the first time. An evangelist named Nigel McNeil came from Australia and spoke at our church, and my mom lined all of us kids up front for him to pray for us. I felt something powerful, and it was good."

After that moment, Leeland says his relationship with God became personal. He listened more at church, prayed more often, started reading his Bible on his own, and tried to soak up everything he could about God. For the next two years, Leeland's family traveled with the Australian evangelist, performing music at his revival meetings around the country. Leeland and his brother sang with their parents, and Leeland began writing songs. After he performed one of his own songs for the first time, he discovered he could communicate God's love through music in a powerful way.

"I closed my eyes and thought about the words that I was singing to God. Halfway through the song, I realized my mom had stopped singing with me. I opened my eyes to see where she was, and she was down at the altar. It was packed with people weeping and crying. My mom was praying for them.

They had come to the altar because the music had reached their hearts.

"I realized in that moment that this was where God wanted to use me. He put that love for music inside me as a tool to use for his kingdom and his glory."

By the time Leeland was fifteen, he had written many songs and was leading worship at church. Then God opened the door for Leeland, his brother, and their band to sign a recording contract and release best-selling CDs like *Love Is on the Move*. The band has been nominated for Grammy Awards, won Dove Awards, and Leeland has written songs for other top Christian artists like Michael W. Smith. In just a few short years, Leeland has shared his love for Jesus all over the world. He recently ministered to the poor in Cambodia with Food for the Hungry. He loves the great adventure he and God are on.

Leeland

continued »

Leeland helping in Cambodia

You can find out more about Leeland and his ministry at leelandonline.com.

"God wants to use you even at a very, very young age," Leeland says. "He wants to use you now. Even at twelve and thirteen and fourteen years old, you might have a lot of dreams in your heart of what you want to do or be, things you love, maybe sports or singing. God put that passion, that desire there so you can use it for him. You don't have to be super talented or super popular. God likes you just the way you are."

Food for the Hungry works in more than twenty-six countries where daily survival is a struggle. The organization helps in the areas of food and agriculture, water and sanitation, health and nutrition, child sponsorship, HIV/AIDS, economic development, church development, and emergency response. Visit fh.org.

 JENNA

So will you open your ears to the cries of this world? More than that, will you open your heart? If we remain closed off—plugged up with headphones, glued to the TV, connected to our cell phones 24/7—we will miss out on the adventure.

> God wants to use you.
> Did you *hear* that?
> The God of the stars and seas wants to use YOU! Will you let him?
> Are you ready to pull the plug?

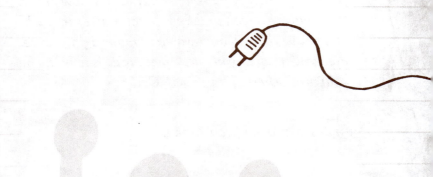

By helping each other with your troubles, you truly obey the law of Christ.

Galatians 6:2

God, I'm scared. I like being plugged. I'm scared to step out of my comfort zone and into the lives of others. Would you give me a new excitement for your children? Would you remind me how much they matter to you and help them matter to me? I don't have the will on my own to make a difference. Please work on my heart. Open my ears to hear the hearts of others. Thank you, God.

In Jesus' name I pray, amen.

CHAPTER 6

20/20

There, at the Temple gate called Beautiful Gate, was a man who had been crippled all his life. . . .

Peter and John looked straight at him and said, "Look at us!" . . . Then Peter took the man's right hand and lifted him up.

Acts 3:2, 4, 7

MAX ⦙⦙⦙

He sat at a Temple gate called Beautiful.

The man was anything but.

He couldn't walk but had to drag himself about on his knees. He passed his days with other beggars who coveted the coins of the worshipers entering Solomon's court.

Peter and John were among them.

The needy man saw the apostles, lifted his voice, and begged for money.

They had none to give, yet still they stopped. "Peter and John looked straight at him and said, 'Look at us!'" (Acts 3:4). They locked their eyes on his with such compassion that "he gave them his attention, expecting to receive something from them" (v. 5 NKJV). Peter and John issued no embarrassed glance, irritated shrug, or instant dismissal but an honest look.

It is hard to look suffering in the face. Wouldn't we rather turn away? Stare in a different direction? Human hurt is not easy on the eye. The dusty cheeks of the Pakistani refugee. The wide-eyed stare of the Haitian orphan. The diseases and disfigurement that can twist even a little child's body. The student who is too large to fit in the desk next to you. The girl in the bathroom crying.

Every person on this planet is one of God's sparrows.

Jesus said, "Two sparrows cost only a penny, but not even one of them can die without your Father's knowing it. God even knows how many hairs are on your head. So don't be afraid. You are worth much more than many sparrows" (Matthew 10:29–31).

Michael Leeland (not to be confused with singer Leeland Mooring) is one of those sparrows.

SPARROW CLUBS USA STORY

Michael Leeland was just six months old when his parents, Jeff and Kristi, found out he needed a bone marrow transplant to save his life. There was only one problem:

The transplant cost $200,000.

And the family's insurance wouldn't pay.

Jeff was a junior high school teacher at the time, and when Dameon, one of Jeff's students, found out about baby Michael, he wanted to help. He emptied his bank account and brought his teacher the entire $60. It was all he had.

Other students heard what Dameon did, and they started to help too. Soon, the whole school was involved. Then the word spread to the local community. In just four weeks, the seed that Dameon planted had grown into $227,000. Baby Michael got his transplant and lived.

But that wasn't the only miracle.

You see, before he gave all he had to help, Dameon was the most picked-on kid at school. "He was twelve years old and weighed 325 pounds. He was in my special ed PE class," Jeff told us.[1] "He started as the target of the school, and at the end-of-the-year school assembly he received the all-school character award and got a five-minute standing ovation. He went from being the outcast to being the hero in just a few weeks. He even told me, 'Mr. Leeland, all of a sudden all these girls want to talk to me!'"

Dameon with Michael

When Jeff realized what a simple act of sacrifice could do—not only for the one who received the gift, but also for the giver—the vision for Sparrow Clubs USA was born. The organization helps match a child in medical crisis with a school that wants to help and community sponsors who will assist with funds needed. Students in Sparrow Clubs earn "Sparrow Cash" by volunteering for community service hours. The Sparrow Cash is turned in to the organization and real funds are sent to the Sparrow's family.

continued »

"I think there are lots of kids who want to make a difference but not many opportunities for kids to exercise that capacity for service," Jeff says. "This is kids helping other kids, and it changes everybody in the process."

Dameon continued to serve Sparrow Clubs until the age of twenty, when he died suddenly of an infection following a surgical procedure. Still, his legacy lives on in Michael, who today is eighteen and in complete remission from his illness. Dameon's legacy continues in the 5 million dollars in assistance that has been given to 650 other sparrows and their families adopted by students in Sparrow Clubs across twenty-six states. And it grows in the changed lives of students who find passion and purpose in their Sparrow Club work.

Sparrow Club members reading to elementary school students.

Students like Brandi Jordan.

"I was a punk all through middle school and almost got held back in eighth grade because I just didn't care," Brandi, now nineteen, admits. "School just wasn't my thing. I got into a lot of trouble. Then I got into high school and they had activity periods where you could either go to a club like the chess club or the Sparrow Club, or you could sit and do homework for an hour. I wasn't about to sit and do homework, so one of my friends and I went to a Sparrow Club meeting to check it out.

"I fell in love with it. I fell in love with what it did. Throughout high school, my life was not so great. My home life was not great. I didn't feel like I had a purpose. It gave me something I could do for someone else, and it felt good."

Brandi went to every club meeting and was involved in every Sparrow activity. In her last two years of high school, she was elected president of her school's Sparrow Club. Since she graduated, she has joined the regional board of directors.

"It totally changed my attitude," she says. "We got to deliver a meal to our Sparrow family once a week, and even that thirty seconds at the door, handing them the food, meant something. They were just so happy, so thankful that we were there. I had a million of those moments, those thirty-second encounters where you knew you were making a difference."

Brandi says finding out she could make a difference helped her get connected to Christ at a summer camp after she graduated from high school. "I went to a rodeo Bible camp and accepted Jesus," Brandi says. "Now I do outreach with my church and I love it. I love sharing God with people."

Sparrow Club members cleaning to earn Sparrow cash.

There are 96,000 public schools in the U.S. and 48 million kids 17 and under who attend those schools. There are also about 9,600 children diagnosed with cancer each year. That means that if just 1 out of every 10 schools started a Sparrow Club, all those sick kids' lives would be changed. (And so would the 500 students' lives at each school.) To start a Sparrow Club at your school or with your home-school group, contact sparrowclubs.org.

Michael. Dameon. Brandi.

Not very beautiful to most people. In fact, Michael's disease, Dameon's weight, and Brandi's attitude were tough to look at. They made you want to turn away. Instead, God drew them all together and healed them with his extravagant love.

When we look at people, what do we see? (Just because you have 20/20 vision doesn't mean you see the way God wants you to see.)

Who are the people you walk right past every day? Pray today that God will help you see them in a whole new way.

Here is some space for you to jot down some thoughts about the people you know that nobody sees. What could make a difference in their lives?

....

....

....

....

....

....

....

....

MAX ||||||||||||||||||||||||||||||||||||||||||||||||||||||||||||||||||||||||||||||||||||||||||||||

There is something fundamentally good about taking time to see a person. Simon the Pharisee once got on Jesus' case about his kindness toward a woman of questionable character. So Jesus tested him: "Do you see this woman?" (Luke 7:44).

Simon didn't. He saw a woman who was anything but pure. He didn't see the woman God made. He missed the masterpiece.

What do we see when we see . . .

→ the people beneath the overpass, around the fire in a fifty-five-gallon drum?
→ the news clips of children in refugee camps?
→ reports of 1.75 billion people who live on less than $1.25 a day?

What do we see? "When He saw the multitudes, He was moved with compassion for them, because they were weary and scattered, like sheep having no shepherd" (Matthew 9:36 NKJV).

Compassion is a movement deep within—a kick in the gut. Maybe that's why we turn away. Who can stand such deep feelings? Especially when we can't do anything about it. Why look suffering in the face if we can't make a difference?

But you can. Your attention can reduce someone's pain.

> If you sit with someone new at lunch today and get to know him or her, it could change both your lives.

This is the promise of the encounter. Brandi took meals to a family whose child was sick. As she did, God reached down and healed her own hurting heart. When she gave, she received even more.

JENNA ～～～～～～～～～～～～～～～～～～

There's always a backstage in someone's heart. Maybe there's a divorce behind the popular girl's pomp. Maybe there's abuse behind the quiet girl's heart who always sits in the back row. That guy who always cracks jokes in class? Maybe he has never met his dad. And that guy that always picks on people? Yeah, maybe he's never been told, "Son, I love you."

Let's try and look behind the mask, behind the popularity, behind the swollen egos, behind the humor or the quietness. Let's make a pact to really get to know people's hearts. The real stuff. Before we judge, let's pray—pray that God will show us how we can love someone better, even when that person is the LAST one we want to love.

Jesus always looked past clothes, social class, gender, and race and focused straight on the heart. When we do that, we see that everyone needs love. Everyone needs Jesus. But who is going to be the person to give that love? I hope it's me. I hope it's you. Let's pray that we see the need and do something about it.

Hearts need healing. In 2006, suicide was the third leading cause of death for young people in the United States ages 15 to 24.

—CDC.gov

Back at the Beautiful Gate, our beggar still can't believe that the apostles stopped to talk to him.

MAX

Then Peter said,

> "Silver and gold I do not have, but what I do have I give you: In the name of Jesus Christ of Nazareth, rise up and walk." And he took him by the right hand and lifted him up, and immediately his feet and ankle bones received strength. So he, leaping up, stood and walked and entered the temple with them—walking, leaping, and praising God. (Acts 3:6–8 NKJV)

What if Peter had said, "Since I don't have any silver or gold, I'll keep my mouth shut"? But he didn't. He placed his mustard-seed-sized deed (a look and a touch) in the soil of God's love. And look what God grew.

The thick, meaty hand of the fisherman reached for the frail, thin one of the beggar. Peter lifted the man toward himself. The cripple swayed like a newborn calf finding its balance. It appeared as if the man would fall, but he didn't. He stood. And as he stood, he began to shout, and passersby began to stop. They stopped and watched the cripple skip.

With God, Peter's adventure gave him power to heal the cripple. The miracle made the crowd sit up and pay attention. Then Peter could tell them about his faith in Christ.

"Repent therefore and be converted, that your sins may be blotted out, so that times of refreshing may come from the presence of the Lord" (v. 19 NKJV).

> "Blotted out" is a translation of a Greek term that means "to obliterate" or "erase completely."
>
> Faith in Christ, Peter explained, leads to a clean slate with God. What Jesus did for the legs of this cripple, he does for our souls. Brand-new!

Peter's honest look led to a helping hand that led to a conversation about eternity.

While you may not be able to heal a crippled person, God's power is still the same today. And he can work through you in lots of ways. To heal hearts, to encourage. To say kind words. To take steps to make someone's life better, easier.

The point is this: works done in God's name long outlive our earthly lives.

JENNA

But we can't do this on our own. This loving-difficult-people thing, this touching the beggar, feeding the homeless, asking the quiet kid at school about his family, or even praying for a chance to get to know the heart of the uppity popular girl who has sneered at you a thousand times. All this is IMPOSSIBLE without God! I don't have the capability to see the hearts of people on my own. I don't even have the desire to do it on my own!

We have to ask God to change our own hearts before we try to change the world. We have to ask God to be our oxygen tank, our life source, our one and only help. When we come to God first—ask him to make our hearts look like him by talking through us, loving through us, and seeing through us—THEN our perspective changes.

Every day becomes an opportunity. An opportunity to encourage, to let Jesus shine through you, to make a difference. Boring algebra homework turns into a chance to tutor the kid who cannot get it.

Studies show that teens who volunteer perform better in school than those who do not.

Practice after school turns into a chance to talk to that guy who wears the same shirt every other day and doesn't have many friends because of poverty. Routine suddenly becomes adventure. God gives us his eyes to see people HIS way.

And when you see people God's way, you see beauty everywhere.

In certain Zulu areas of South Africa, people greet each other with a phrase that means "I see you."[2]

Change begins with a genuine look.

And continues with a helping hand.

Could this be God's strategy for human hurt? First, kind eyes meet desperate ones. Next, strong hands help weak ones. Then, the miracle of God.

We do our small part,
he does the big part,
and life at the Beautiful Gate begins to be just that.

When he arrived, he saw a great crowd waiting. He felt sorry for them, because they were like sheep without a shepherd.

Mark 6:34

Father, in Genesis 16:13 you are called "God who sees me," and I know that your eyes are always looking out for me and guiding me. You have given me eyes, too, and I ask that you would help me REALLY see, to see with your eyes. Help me see those you put in my path in a new way—see their hurts, their desires, their longings, their needs, their joys, and their challenges. And as you open my eyes, open my arms. I want to love and serve people like Jesus did. Make me like you, God.

In Jesus' name I pray, amen.

CHAPTER 7

STAND UP FOR THE HAVE-NOTS

Then the King will say, "I'm telling the solemn truth: Whenever you did one of these things to someone overlooked or ignored, that was me—you did it to me."

Matthew 25:40 MSG

Think back to the day you were born. . . .

Okay, so you may not remember it, but you've probably heard the details. You weighed a few pounds and a certain number of ounces. You were a number of inches long. You were bald or had lots of dark hair or a little blonde peach fuzz. You most likely were born in a hospital with plenty of trained medical attendants and top-of-the-line equipment standing by to make sure you got off to the best start.

The doctor cleared your airway and you took your first breath.

"Waaahhh!" you wailed in surprise. Then you were quickly swaddled in warm blankets and placed in loving arms.

Welcome to the world, son.

We have everything ready for you, daughter.

If you are growing up in North America, especially in the United States or Canada, you've most likely had a roof over your head, food on the table, and clothes to wear every day of your life. You've had a bedroom with lots of stuff in it, hot showers and medicines, games and toys, and trips to fun places.

Congratulations!

If you are going to live on Planet Earth, you sure picked the right address—even though you didn't pick it at all. See, according to a United Nations Human Development Report, three quarters of the world's income goes to 20 percent of the world's population.[1] And that 20 percent is mostly us.

Numbers are hard to see, so try this word picture.

JENNA ～～～～～～～～～～～～～～～～～～～～～～～

Let's say your local Apple store is giving out ten free iPods to the first students who get in line the next day. The next morning, the first ten anxious Apple lovers file in line. But instead of the Apple store handing out one iPod per person, the first two students in line get *eight* iPods, while the other eight students have to take turns sharing two. Does that seem fair?

The ones who got four iPods each could easily say, "Well, I deserve all of these because I am a really nice person and work really hard to make straight A's." But let's get out of this fantasy situation and stare real life in the face. What if we asked this question about the world: Why do a few of us have so much in this world while most have so little? And better still—what does God want us to do about it?

I think he wants us to make a big deal about poverty! God

mentions poverty again and again in Scripture. Usually when God says something more than once in the Bible, our ears should stand at attention. The poor are important to God. And what is important to God should be important to us. It's time we serve the have-nots. God calls the have-nots the "least of these" in Matthew 25:40 (NIV).

~~~~~~

Read what Jesus says in Matthew 25:31–40.

Who does he say will be gathered before him?

....

....

....

What will he say to the people on his right? What did the people on the King's right do for the hungry, thirsty, and the stranger?

....

....

....

....

....

Verses 37–40 tell how the people on the right reply:

Then the good people will answer, "Lord, when did we see you hungry and give you food, or thirsty and give you something to drink? When did we see you alone and away from home and invite you into our house? When did we see you without clothes and give you something to wear? When did we see you sick or in prison and care for you?"

Then the King will answer, "I tell you the truth, anything you did for even the least of my people here, you also did for me."

What does the King say to the people on his left (v. 41)?

....

....

....

....

....

....

Ouch! When it's time to meet Jesus, which side do you want to be on?

The *right* side, of course.

God takes the lives of the poor so seriously that he mentions them again and again in his Word.

Jim Wallis once took some scissors to his Bible. (We don't recommend this.) He was a seminary student at Trinity Evangelical Divinity School when he and some classmates decided to eliminate a few verses. They performed surgery on all sixty-six books, beginning with Genesis and not stopping until Revelation.

Each time a verse mentioned poverty, wealth, justice, or oppression, they cut it out. They wanted to see what a compassionless Bible looked like. By the time they finished, nearly two thousand verses lay on the floor![2]

Cut concern for the poor out of the Bible and you cut the heart out of it. God makes the poor his priority. When the hungry pray, he listens. When orphans cry, he sees.—ML

JENNA

Her name is Chaltu. She is fourteen years old. She loves to hang out with her friends and hates her chores, loves going to school but stresses over having no time to do homework. She dreams of becoming a singer and getting out of her small hometown so she can see the world.

What makes her different from the average American teen? Let's go down this list:

1. Chaltu lives in a mud hut in Ethiopia.
2. She takes care of her grandmother full-time because her parents died. (Take your chores and multiply the difficulty by 100. With no electricity, no bleach, and no

washer/dryer, you can only imagine how hard her chores are!)

3. Whereas we might not finish homework due to a tennis tournament, choir competition, or just hanging out with friends too much, Chaltu cannot finish her homework because of water. Water? Yes. It takes a full day to walk to the watering hole—the same watering hole that camels and monkeys drink from—fill up heavy jugs of water, and make the long trek home.

4. Her idea of seeing the world is to travel to the nearest town (Nazaret, a twenty-minute drive away). She can only dream about this because cars are a novelty and roads are scarce.

The major thing that makes my life different from Chaltu's is my birthplace. I also hated chores, dreamed of becoming a rock star, wanted to see the world, and stressed about school. BUT I grew up in America—the land of opportunity, dreams that come true, roofs over heads, closets crammed full, and clean running water. Chaltu was born in a country where baths and shoes are luxuries, dreams turn into nightmares when parents die, and it is a daily struggle to survive.

When I think of the have-nots I need to have a heart for, I think of Chaltu.

Dad thinks of Dadhi.

Jenna and Chaltu

Photo:
©Jon Warren/
World Vision 2010

MAX ||||||||||||||||||||||||||||||||||||||||||||||||||||||||||||||||||||||||||||||||||||||||||||||||||||||||||||||

I spent time thinking about this one morning on the Ethiopian farm of Dadhi. Dadhi is a sturdy but struggling husband and father. His dirt-floored mud hut would fit easily in my garage. His wife's handwoven baskets decorate his walls. Straw mats are rolled and stored against the sides, awaiting nightfall when all seven family members will sleep on them. Dadhi's five children smile quickly and hug tightly. They don't know how poor they are.

Dadhi does.

He earns less than a dollar a day at a nearby farm.

He'd work his own land, except a plague took the life of his ox.

His only one.

With no ox, he can't plow. With no plowed field, he can't sow a crop. If he can't sow a crop, he can't harvest one.

All he needs is an ox.

Oxen are very useful to farmers. They help plant and harvest their own "fuel" (think about it), work well in hilly areas that a tractor can't navigate, and can work soil that is too wet for machines. They also cost less than machines and don't break down as often.

Dadhi is energetic and industrious. He has mastered a trade and been faithful to his wife. He's committed no crimes. Neighbors respect him. He seems every bit as intelligent as

I am, likely more so. He and I share the same attributes and dreams. I listed them on this chart.

ATTRIBUTES	DADHI	MAX
Physically able	X	X
Willing to work	X	X
Trained to do a job	X	X
Loves family	X	X
Sober and drug free	X	X
Good reputation	X	You tell me

We have a lot in common.

And you don't have to travel sixteen hours in a plane to find a Dadhi or two. They live in the nursing home you pass on the way to church. They gather at the gas station on the corner. They hang out after school at the bowling alley or the mall. They are the poor, the brokenhearted, the homeless, the friends with dysfunctional families, the people with addictions, and the people who are blind to the love God has for them.

South Dakota's Pine Ridge Reservation, home to about 75,000 Native Americans of the Oglala Sioux Tribe, is the poorest community in America. Almost half the homes on the reservation have no working toilets or telephones. Alcoholism is rampant, the dropout rate is more than 70 percent, and suicide is five times higher than the U.S.

national average. During a recent blizzard, a
few people actually froze to death because
of lack of heat and blankets. Wings as Eagles
Ministries works in many ways on the
reservation to raise the standard of living
and introduce people to Christ. If you want
to help by donating funds, getting a work
team together to serve at the reservation, or
praying for the enormous needs of Pine
Ridge, visit WAEministries.com.

Now that God has opened your eyes to the needs around you, where do you start?

Let's go back to the first church.

In those early days, the church grew so fast that it soon found needy people in its midst. Some of them were widows—women whose husbands had died. They had no source of income. No government support or company retirement fund. According to the culture of their day, the extended family provided support. But extended families didn't approve of their new beliefs and disowned them, leaving these widows who had decided to follow Jesus with only one place to turn . . . their new church.

What did the church do?

The congregation responded with a daily distribution of food, clothing, and money.

That's it.

Sounds simple, doesn't it?

Everyone shared what they already had.

Every day.

Can you start there with what you've already got? You have discovered many of your skills and talents and God-given gifts. Now take a look around you at the resources you have.

Got any money saved up?

Do you earn or receive money regularly?

How about extra clothes, shoes, room decorations, and food that you could share?

Gift cards you haven't used?

Okay, here's a good one: how about free time after school, on the weekends, and on school breaks?

Teens and youth in the United States collected 625,000 pairs of jeans during Do Something's recent Teens for Jeans campaign; 200,000 of which went to youth in Haiti.

—DoSomething.org

Why don't you brainstorm a little? Feel free to doodle on this page any thoughts you have on the resources already at your fingertips. When you are willing to give what you have, God can do marvelous things with it. In the book of Matthew, Jesus takes a few loaves of bread and small fish and feeds a huge crowd not once, but *two* times. In Matthew 14, he feeds five thousand people with five loaves and two fish.

Then in Matthew 15, he feeds four thousand people with seven loaves and a few fish. In both stories, there were baskets of leftovers.

Could God take your offering of gently used sweaters, blankets, and some new socks and multiply them to keep people warm? (*Easy as pie.*)

Would he take food you collect and use it to bless a lot more people than you thought you could feed? (*Just his cup of tea.*)

Can he take a simple relationship you start with a lonely peer and expand your circle of friends for a lifetime? (*Piece of cake.*)

And every time you give, the blessing comes right back to you. (*That's the icing on the cake. With sprinkles on top.*)

Just one question: are you hungry yet?

Hungry to play your part in Jesus' to-do list for this world?

MAX

> The Spirit of the LORD is upon Me, because He has anointed Me to preach the gospel to the poor; He has sent Me to heal the brokenhearted. To proclaim liberty to the captives and recovery of sight to the blind, to set at liberty those who are oppressed; to proclaim the acceptable year of the LORD.
> (Luke 4:18–19 NKJV)

→ Heal the brokenhearted.
→ Proclaim liberty to the captives.
→ Restore sight to the blind.
→ Set free those who are oppressed.
→ And proclaim the acceptable year of the Lord.

Here's what's cool about that last part. "Acceptable year of the Lord" reminded the people of the year of Jubilee, a twice-in-every-hundred-years celebration that God used to press the restart button on the machinery of justice.

JUBILATION *(noun):* 1. an act of rejoicing; 2. an expression of great joy

—Merriam-Webster.com

The year of Jubilee went like this: Beginning on the Day of Atonement, all the fields were allowed to rest. No farming was permitted. For a year, the land could recover from the previous forty-nine years of planting and harvesting. Another benefit of the year of Jubilee was that all property was returned to its original owners. In this agricultural society, land was their investment, their savings. Families could lose their land through tragedy, sickness, or even laziness. The Jubilee provision guaranteed that every family, at least twice a century, would have the opportunity to get back on its feet.

In addition, all the slaves were freed. Anyone who had been sold into slavery or who had sold himself into slavery to pay off debt was released.

Woo-hoo! Fertile soil again. No more debt. Fortune returned. Bondage ended.

Create your own Jubilee season. Forgive a debt that someone owes you. Return any items you borrowed and forgot about (a friend's favorite shirt, a library book, your sister's hairbrush). While you are at it, get rid of any grudges you've been carrying around. Let them go and forgive those who have hurt you. If you know someone is holding a grudge against you, do whatever you can to make the relationship better. Then celebrate!

Wouldn't it be great if we had a year of Jubilee and all the slaves around the world today were freed?

What?

You didn't know there were any slaves left in the world? You thought Abraham Lincoln ended that a long time ago? Actually, there were more than 28.4 million slaves at the end of 2006, according to researcher Siddharth Kara; and Kara believes the number is growing.[3] They deserve to be free. Just talk to eighteen-year-old, modern-day slavery fighter (otherwise known as an *abolitionist*, but we don't need the fancy word) Zach Hunter.

ZACH'S STORY

"The first time I heard about slavery was when I was twelve years old," Zach told us.[4] "It was February, which is Black History Month, and I was learning about some of the most amazing men and women who ever lived: activists and abolitionists, those who fought for their own freedom and the freedom of others.

"In my mind, slavery is the single most embarrassing thing in the history of America—that people would think it was okay to own someone based on the color of their skin really ticked me off. I wished that I had been born back then so I

continued »

could have done something about it. I came home and talked to my mom about it, and found out there were twenty-seven million people in physical bondage around the world, doing someone else's work, being used as sex slaves, making my clothes, making chocolate for me to consume in America. It infuriated me, and it became my passion. I kept thinking about it. It was eating my lunch!

"My first thought was, 'What can I do?' If I was in slavery, I would want someone to free me. It's as simple as that."

Zach came up with the idea that students at his school could collect change and donate it to help end slavery. "Loose Change to Loosen Chains" (LC2LC) began. Today, kindergarten through high school students all over the world launch LC2LC campaigns, and International Justice Mission uses the donated funds to free modern-day slaves.

"I told my parents that I wanted to raise money and tell people about this, and then I talked to my principal," Zach says. "I asked him if I could speak to the student body. I was terrified. I was scared to death to speak in front of people I knew. I'm sure I was even more pale than usual. But I just got

Zach Hunter speaking about slavery to more than 1,000 teens

up there and delivered my message, and the response was incredible.

"The amazing thing was that the classes who gave the most were the kindergarten, first grade, and second graders. Some people don't want a first grader to hear about the realities of slavery; it's too painful. But you can talk about it on an age-appropriate level, and they want to help in a big way."

Zach's passion to tell others about the issue opened doors for him to speak at the White House. It also took him on a summer tour of Christian music festivals, where he promoted the film *Amazing Grace*, the story of William Wilberforce, the man who led the fight to make slavery illegal in Britain. Then Zach put his message to motivate teens on paper, writing books called *Be the Change, Generation Change*, and *Lose Your Cool*.

"I think a lot of my generation is interested in making a difference, but we have to have passion," Zach says. "For me, the difference between interest and passion is action. I describe it as a fire in my bones that doesn't allow me to look the other way. And your passion has to come from God to be constructive. Hitler was one of the most passionate people who ever lived, but his passion was so destructive, so evil. It [helpful passion] has to come from God, and I think he gives that freely if you just ask for it."

God loves it when we have a passion to level the playing field. To welcome the have-nots and the little guys onto the team.

He wants us to combine our skills and resources so we can win the ultimate World Series for him.

Are we hitting home runs yet?

Not enough to achieve total victory.

Now it's true that some people are poor because they are lazy. They need to get off their duffs. Others, however, are poor because parasites weaken their bodies, because they spend six hours a day collecting water, because rebel armies ravaged their farms, or because AIDS took their parents. Couldn't those people use a bit of Jubilee? A little loose change to loosen chains?

Of course they could. So . . .

Let the church act on behalf of the poor. The apostles did. "So the Twelve called a meeting of all the believers" (Acts 6:2 NLT). They assembled the entire church. The leaders wanted every member to know that this church took poverty seriously. The ultimate solution to poverty is found in the compassion of God's people. Scripture points to Spirit-led volunteerism among God's people.

Here's another idea. Like Zach when he heard about modern-day slaves, *Get ticked off*. That's right. Get mad enough to respond. Righteous anger would do a world of good. Poverty is not the lack of charity but the lack of justice. Why do a billion people go to bed hungry every night?[5] Why do nearly thirty thousand children die every day, one every three seconds, from hunger and preventable diseases?[6]

One, one thousand;

Two, one thousand;

Three . . . It's just not fair.

What does your church do to help the poor? If you don't know, use your investigative skills and find out! You could call the church office, make an appointment to talk to your minister, or grab some face time with your youth leader. Ask how your church helps in your community, in your country, around the world. People near and far who have lost everything in storms or floods or fires. People with families and no income. People who are hungry or have medical needs.

What did you discover?

....

....

....

....

....

....

Now comes the exciting part. How can you get involved? What are some ways you could do more?

Maybe your church or youth group could . . .

➡ Have a garage sale and use the money raised to buy an ox, cow, sheep, or goat for a family in another country.

➡ Sell pancake breakfasts or spaghetti dinners before the next church function.

➡ Collect jackets and blankets for the homeless. Or for children who need jackets, gloves, and hats in local schools or shelters.

➡ Volunteer to feed the homeless at a local soup kitchen.

➡ Become a distribution center for the Angel Food program (Angelfoodministries.com). For a low cost, families can buy a large box of healthy foods for four people.

➡ Invite orphans—or foster teens—who will be on their own soon to become part of your church family.

Many hospitals still accept teen volunteers, some as young as 12 or 13. The traditional name for a hospital volunteer is a "candy striper," because the uniform often consists of a striped shirt or apron for volunteers to wear. Candy stripers answer telephones, check visitors in, and give directions to different departments.

What ideas do you have? List a few starting points here.

1. ....

2. ....

3. ....

4. ....

Heifer International was started more than sixty years ago by Dan West, whose heart was touched after he handed out milk to hungry children during the Spanish Civil War. He didn't have enough milk for all of them, so he literally had to decide who would live and who would die. He knew that if these poor families only had a cow, they could feed themselves. Today, Heifer has helped more than 8.5 million people in 125 countries. You can donate a cow, a goat, a flock of geese or ducks, and even knitting baskets. You can give as little as $20 to help buy a flock of chicks or as much as $10,000 for a whole livestock development program. Check out Heifer.org to learn more. This Web site is packed with great fund-raising ideas to help you get started.

MAX

Let the brightest among us lead us. "And so, brothers, select seven men who are well respected and are full of the Spirit and wisdom. We will give them this responsibility" (Acts 6:3 NLT).

The apostles unleashed their best people on their biggest problem. The challenge demands this. Simple solutions simply don't exist. As a young person, you probably don't know what to do about the avalanche of national debt, the lack of life-saving medicines, the corruption at the seaports, and the kidnapping and slavery of children. Most adults don't know what to do, but someone does!

Some people are pouring every ounce of their God-given wisdom into the resolution of these problems, and you could be one of them. We need our brightest and best to continue the legacy of the Jerusalem task force of Acts 6.

Can you take those smarts you are blessed with and work a little harder in school? Learn more than is required? Go deeper? Why not make it your goal to soak up everything you can in the areas where you are gifted? You have gifts to share that someone else needs. If you don't hone your skills, someone may miss out on your solution.

JENNA

A lot of middle school girls are sick of the drama but don't do anything about it. Samantha and Kaylee decided to be different. They are sisters in seventh and eighth grade who began a Bible study, once a week, right after school. Not only is it giving other girls encouragement and perspective, but also it's been a chance for Samantha and Kaylee to finally agree on something in life! (Sisters have their own drama too.)

David, an eighth grader who attends my church, lost his mom in a car accident not too long ago. But instead of hating God and hating life because his mom is gone, David has used his story as a chance to share God and spread TRUE life. The week of his mom's death, he spoke in front of his peers on his school campus. He said that his only hope is Jesus Christ and that his mom lives in heaven. David then told them that if they wanted to know Jesus, they could talk to him about it.

David used his story. Samantha and Kaylee used their problems. They jumped on the opportunities they were given in order to make a difference.

No one can do everything, but everyone can do something.

Some people can fast and pray. Others can study and speak out.

> For just about a dollar a day, you can change the life of a child forever by sponsoring a child through organizations like World Vision or Compassion. They offer food, training, tutoring, the gospel, and more to children in need all over the world. Just $35–$38 a month means giving up one soft drink, candy bar, or pack of gum a day. Visit WorldVision.org or Compassion.com.

What about you? Get out of your comfort zone. Why not teach a Bible study after school? Use your vacation to build houses in hurricane-ravaged towns? Run for student government? Help raise money for a farmer to get an ox?

Speaking of which, I received a note from Dadhi the other day. It included a photo of him and a new family member. A new three-hundred-pound, four-legged family member—an ox. Both of them were smiling. I'm thinking God was too.

Dadhi with his oxen

Photo:
©Jon Warren/
World Vision 2010

Pure and genuine religion in the sight of God the Father means caring for orphans and widows in their distress and refusing to let the world corrupt you.

James 1:27 NLT

Dear Lord, Jesus promised that we would always have the poor among us. Help me make sure that the reverse is also true, that I am always among the poor—helping, encouraging, and lending a hand wherever I can. Give me ideas and compassion to help the poor. I get so busy and me-focused in my little world. Would you open my eyes to loving the homeless with the gifts you have given me? Use me to spread your love and hope to the poor and maybe even reduce their numbers. I love you, Jesus. Thank you for being the Great Provider. Bless the poor today.

In Jesus' name I pray, amen.

CHAPTER 8

WHEN TO PUT UP YOUR DUKES

A thief comes to steal and kill and destroy, but I came to give life—life in all its fullness.

John 10:10

Ladies and gentlemen, in this corner of the ring, the challenger, "Plain Cheese Pizza."

Sixteen inches in diameter.
Crispy around the edges.
Soft and squishy in the middle—but boy, is he hot!

And in the opposite corner, we have the defending heavyweight champion, "The Enemy."

Sixteen feet tall,
covered with steely scales,
stinking of sulphur and breathing fire,
The Enemy is ready to take little doughboy down.

If you want to make a real difference in the world for Jesus, get ready for a fight. Because ever since God condemned Satan to hell (check out Revelation 12), he's been determined to take as many of God's masterpieces with him as he can. He's determined to pay God back, and what better way to hurt the Creator than to destroy the most beautiful things he's made? (That's us.)

Pretty heavy stuff, isn't it?

Making a difference for God on this fallen planet is serious, supernatural business. If you've made a life commitment to Jesus, Satan can't get you in the end. We already know who wins the championship title, and he's in your corner. But if you're messing with the devil's plans to bring other people down, he will definitely try to rough you up. Punch your spiritual lights out.

If you plan to be the change for Christ, prepare for persecution.

We know what you're thinking: *Hold up. Wait just a minute. Persecution? Are you serious? Personally, I like my comfort zone.*

That's what the enemy is counting on. One of the best tricks he's got up his sleeve is to take your initial enthusiasm for God, the fire inside you to change the world, and spray a garden hose on those flames of forward motion until you come to a sopping, sputtering stop. He slithers over to your ear and hisses, "This is too hard. You'll never be able to do this." "No one cares about this stuff but you, and you can't do it by yourself." "Come on, you don't really want to give up your weekend to do this, do you?"

> The Bible calls Satan "the dragon" and says believers in Christ are in a war with him. (Revelation 12:17)

He'll try to get you any way he can. And he's good at it too. He'll shake your self-confidence or puff you up with pride. He'll say you're too young, too short, too skinny, too unpopular, too *anything* to keep you plugged up with headphones instead of getting your gloves on and stepping into the ring to fight. Fight for others. Fight for people who need you. Fight for people who need Jesus. He'll convince you you're bored or distract you with electronics. He'll make you think your ideas are stupid or impossible.

> The typical American teen spends more than five hours a day watching television, DVDs, surfing the Net, or playing video games. The average teen also sends and receives 96 text messages daily.
>
> —Nielsen[1]

Show the devil you mean business when it comes to devoting time to develop your spiritual muscles. Here are three classic Christian authors whose works should challenge you:

1. Oswald Chambers (*My Utmost for His Highest*)
2. C. S. Lewis (Go beyond the Chronicles of Narnia. Try *Mere Christianity*.)
3. Francis Schaeffer (*How Should We Then Live?*)

But you know what?

God loves the impossible. Because with God "all things are possible" (Matthew 19:26).

JENNA ⌇⌇⌇⌇⌇⌇⌇⌇⌇⌇⌇⌇⌇⌇⌇⌇⌇⌇⌇⌇⌇

Okay, so I may sound like a broken record here, but seriously, you can't change the world alone. The impossible can only be made possible through a supernatural God.

My sister Sara was only nineteen years old when she went to India on a mission trip. One afternoon, Sara and some of her team went to a family's house to share the gospel. After they told the Hindu-believing family about Jesus, the family was eager to accept this new hope. Yet I'm sure they were also slightly hesitant.

To destroy any doubt of the power of Jesus Christ, the mission team asked if any family member had an ailment that they could pray for. Sure enough, the grandmother admitted to excruciating back pain that had left her hunched over. The team gathered around her, laid hands on her, and began to pray in the name of the God who makes ALL things possible. Faithfully, God answered their prayers and healed the grandmother's back instantly. Her eyes brightened, her shoulders straightened, and she began to laugh and even dance around!

You serve a God who can heal through you, serve through you, be patient through you, even do the impossible through you.

⌇⌇⌇⌇⌇⌇⌇⌇⌇⌇⌇⌇⌇⌇⌇⌇⌇⌇⌇⌇⌇⌇⌇⌇⌇⌇⌇⌇⌇⌇⌇⌇

God *wants* to do the impossible through you, but sometimes we confuse "possible" with "easy." It isn't easy, comfortable, or fun to serve God all the time. Sometimes it's downright hard. It may go something like this:

➡ Heidi is the only believer on her high school cheerleading squad. When the others go wild after games, she goes home. When they party on road trips, she goes to her room.

→ Jeff's classmates give him a hard time because he doesn't text a friend for a test answer and won't text an answer to someone else.

→ Maria's friends laugh at her when she refuses to buy a bikini when they are shopping for swimsuits.

→ Nathan doesn't feel like going to his volunteer commitment to help fix up a house today. He's going to miss a paintball game.

→ Ashley wants to keep her pledge to remain sexually pure before marriage, but it's not easy because her friends don't have the same goal.

Nope, it's not easy standing out from the crowd for Jesus, is it? But when we fall in love with him and want to share that love with the world, we can expect to face some opposition.

> *"I have found the paradox that if I love until it hurts, then there is no hurt, but only more love."*
>
> —Mother Teresa

While we may feel picked on or left out, in some places of the world, Christ-followers face real danger.

Xu Yonghai, a Christian in Communist China, worked to try to get the government to make house churches (sometimes called "underground churches") legal. The government responded by locking him in a Beijing prison for two years. His cell was eight-by-eight feet. There was no bathroom, only a pipe in a corner from which water flowed onto the concrete. "My cell was the last stop for prisoners sentenced to die," he said. "At times there were as many as three other prisoners in the tiny, damp room, awaiting their date with the executioner."

Yonghai survived through prayer, meditation, and writing. On the walls of his cell, he wrote, with a bar of soap, the major points for a book about God. Once he finished, he memorized all those thoughts. After he was released, he turned his prison thoughts into a fifty-thousand-word book called *God the Creator*.[2]

RIFQA'S STORY

Rifqa Bary believes that she worships at her own risk. The eighteen-year-old emigrated as a child with her family from Sri Lanka and converted from Islam to Christianity in her early teens. She had to hide her Bible and sneak out of her parents' home to go to Bible studies. In 2009, when she was seventeen, she ran away from her home in Ohio to a pastor's home in Florida, fearing her devout Muslim parents would harm her or disown her for becoming a Christian. She was also afraid that if her family moved back or sent her back to Sri Lanka, she would be killed for her beliefs. She entered the foster care system rather than return home and asked the court system not to send her back to her family. Her fear of persecution drew national attention from all kinds of news media.

"In 150 generations in my family, no one has known Jesus. I am the first—imagine the honor in killing me," Rifqa said in a YouTube interview.

Now you probably won't be disowned by your family or hurt by them for believing in Jesus. But family members or friends might make fun of your beliefs. Teachers may criticize your convictions. Classmates could snicker at your choices.

So when the going gets tough—okay, not tough like Yonghai or Rifqa had it, but uncomfortable or frustrating—how can we prepare ourselves? Just like they did. Yonghai chased after the presence of Jesus and found strength. Rifqa stood up to her own parents in order to honor Jesus. Courage comes as we think about the accomplishments of Christ.

How have you been persecuted for your faith in Christ?

....

....

....

....

What did you do? Did you back down or come out swinging?

....

....

....

....

Boxing was a sport mentioned as far back as 675 BC in Homer's Illiad.[3]

It's simple. You can take the enemy's punches and remain standing if you . . .

 MAX ||||||||||||||||||||||||||||||||||||||||||||||||||||||||||||||||||||||||||||||||||||||||||||||||||||

Imitate the disciples.

Keep chasing after Jesus.
Keep your relationship with him up-to-date.
Think about how much you are loved.
Memorize his words.
Talk to him.

Courage comes as we live with Jesus.

Peter said it this way: "Don't give the opposition a second thought. Through thick and thin, keep your hearts at attention, in adoration before Christ, your Master. Be ready to speak up and tell anyone who asks why you're living the way you are, and always with the utmost courtesy" (1 Peter 3:14–15 MSG).

Check out this three-strand plan for keeping your relationship with God in fighting shape:

1. Read the Bible daily.
2. Hang with friends and mentors who like Jesus too.
3. Pray a lot.

The three-fold approach works great because if you take three individual pieces of string and pull on the ends hard enough, the strings will snap in two. But if you take those three pieces of string and braid them together, the braid is much harder to break. Together, the string is a lot stronger than its individual parts. When you strengthen your faith all three ways, it's harder for the enemy to defeat you.

And if anyone knew about persecution, it was the apostles.

Peter and John can tell you. They healed the cripple one minute and faced harassment the next. "Now as they [Peter and John] spoke to the people, the priests, the captain of the temple, and the Sadducees came upon them, being greatly disturbed that they taught the people and preached in Jesus the resurrection from the dead" (Acts 4:1–2 NKJV).

Before this, the early church had enjoyed smooth sailing. The Pentecost miracle brought in three thousand followers. The church overflowed with acts of kindness, compassion, and fellowship. Their good deeds showed everyone the truth of their good news. The first three chapters of Acts are happy days. But then comes Acts 4. The church is barely born, and in walk the town bullies: "the priests, the captain of the temple, and the Sadducees came upon them" (v. 1).

A brawny soldier presses through the crowd. He wears heavy ringlets of shoulder-length hair. His naked chest bulges, and his massive legs seem to be poured iron. A medallion of authority hangs on his chest, and he carries a whip in his hand. He can, by law, arrest anyone who transgresses the temple courts. He has come to enforce the law.

The priests follow him: Caiaphas and his father-in-law, Annas. They stand on either side of the temple captain and cross their arms and glare this implicit warning: "Don't forget what we did to your Messiah. Didn't the three spikes on the Roman cross make it clear?"

Annas, the high priest, arches an eyebrow in the direction of Peter. He has not forgotten what this apostle did to his servant a handful of weeks ago in the Garden of Gethsemane. When the servant and the soldiers came to arrest Jesus, Peter drew his sword and "struck the high priest's servant, and cut off his right ear" (John 18:10 NKJV). Jesus healed the ear, but the high priest has not forgotten the incident. I can imagine Annas tugging his ear and menacing, "I have a score to settle with you, Peter."

Peter, meanwhile, may be wrestling with a few Thursday night memories of his own. Not just about his slashing sword, but also his dashing feet. He and the other followers scooted out of the garden like scalded puppies, leaving Jesus to face his foes all alone. Later that night Peter mustered up enough loyalty to appear at Jesus' trial. But when people recognized him, Peter wilted again. He denied his Savior, not once, but three times. So far the score is Persecution–2, Peter–0. Peter has failed every test of persecution. But he won't fail this one.

"Apostle" comes from the Greek word apostolos, which means "messenger" or "one sent forth."

The trio stands firm. If their legs tremble, it's because the beggar just learned to stand and the apostles are choosing not to run. Peter, filled with the Holy Spirit, said to them, "Rulers of the people and elders of Israel: If we this day are judged for a good deed done to a helpless man, by what means he has been made well, let it be known to you all, and to all the people of Israel, that by the name of Jesus Christ of Nazareth, whom you crucified, whom God raised from the dead, by Him this man stands here before you whole" (Acts 4:8–10 NKJV).

No back down in those words.

Annas and Caiaphas snarl. The temple captain squeezes his whip. The eyes of the Sadducees narrow into tiny slits. They glare at Peter and John. But the apostles don't budge an inch. What has happened to them?

Luke gives us the answer in verse 13: "Now when [the accusers] saw the boldness of Peter and John, and perceived that they were uneducated and untrained men, they marveled. And they realized that they had been with Jesus."

Peter and John had been with Jesus. The Jesus who came back to life. The resurrected Jesus. In the Upper Room when he walked through the wall. Standing next to Thomas when the disciple touched the wounds. On the beach when Jesus cooked the fish. Sitting at Jesus' feet for forty days as he explained the ways of the kingdom.

They had spent a long time in the presence of the resurrected King. Awakening with him, listening to him, walking with him. And because they had, this time they could not be silent. "We cannot but speak the things which we have seen and heard" (v. 20).

We didn't walk on earth before Jesus died on the cross. We can only know the Jesus who has already conquered death. We can have a personal relationship with the living

King of kings. We can read his Word, talk to him, and spend time with him. Then we can take on the enemy and knock him out cold.

 MAX |||||||||||||||||||||||||||||||||||||||||||||||||||||||||||||||||||||||||||||||||||||||||||||||||||||||||||||||||||||||||||

Be with Jesus today. Be in his Word. Be with other people who love him. Be in his presence. And when persecution comes (and it will), be strong.

Who knows? People may realize that you, like the disciples, have been with Christ.

|||||||||||||||||||||||||||||||||||||||||||||||||||||||||||||||||||||||||||||||||||||||||||

> Put on the full armor of God so that you can fight against the devil's evil tricks.
> (from Ephesians 6:11)

The power of the wicked will be broken, but the LORD supports those who do right.

Psalm 37:17

Father, none of us likes to think about persecution. And we sure don't like to experience it! Yet in your wisdom and grace, you warn us that persecution is coming. You tell us these things not to alarm us but to prepare us for what's ahead—so that we might endure and persevere and also that these hard experiences would glorify you and benefit us.

Help me see the world through your eyes by focusing on your Son, remembering what he accomplished on the cross despite the persecution heaped on him. Whatever persecution I might suffer, Lord, let it bring you honor—and use it to help other followers of Jesus who will face their own persecution.

In Jesus' name I pray, amen.

PART 3

YOU WERE MADE TO CHANGE THE WORLD

Some people, by always continuing to do good, live for God's glory, for honor, and for life that has no end.
—Romans 2:7

"Find a need and fill it."
—Ruth Stafford Peale

Sponsor a child . . . make bracelets to earn sponsor fee.

MAKE ME YOUR HANDS AND FEET TODAY, JESUS.

Miss Jones broke her arm . . . rake the leaves in her yard.

The Children's Home soccer team needs T-shirts . . . organize youth group to design and supply shirts.

CHAPTER 9

WHEN A WHOLE GENERATION SAYS GO!

Now all who believed were together.

Acts 2:44 NKJV

If you sat down with a pen and a pad of paper and started writing down names, how many of your family members could you list? A mom, dad, grandparents, aunts, uncles, or cousins? Extended cousins, twice removed, on your father's brother's uncle's side? Great-Auntie Ella Jay or Great-Uncle Horace? How about a stepmom or stepdad? Brothers and sisters?

Who are the people related to you?

List your immediate family members here.

....

....

Who has the funniest or most interesting name in your family?

....

Who are you the closest to?

....

Who else is in your family?

You might be surprised.

Arkansas couple Jim Bob and Michelle Duggar have 19 children (so far), and all the kids' names start with the letter J. Talk about a big family!

Whether you have so many cousins you haven't met them all or you can count your immediate family members on one hand, your whole family is actually a lot bigger than you think. See, once you follow Christ, you have family members all over the world. In every country and every kind of circumstance. Of every color and every kind of background.

In a study by the Associated Press and MTV, 1,280 people ages 13 to 24 ranked spending time with family as the number-one thing that made them happy.

You have millions of brothers and sisters in Christ. They are poor, rich, tall, short. They are elementary school kids and high schoolers. College students and grocery store workers. Heads of state and chairmen of big corporations. They are all around you, and that's amazing—because there's some serious power in numbers. And power is a good thing when you want to make a difference.

Your eyes are now opened. You feel terrible about all the needs that are not being met around the world. You want your classmates' lives to be better. You want every person on earth to have enough to eat. You want prejudice and slavery to stop. You want sicknesses to be treated. You want everyone to hear about Jesus.

You really do want to make a difference.

And you can.
And you will.

And you probably already are.

But do you want to make a really BIG difference? Beyond-your-wildest-dreams BIG?

A million-dollar difference like Austin Gutwein or a save-people-from-slavery difference like Zach Hunter? A bloom-where-you're-planted difference like Jessica Woolbright and thousands of other teens like you?

Of course you do.

Then it's time to call a family meeting. A family reunion,

if you will. Yep. You can get with the friends, family members, youth group, or classmates who also love Jesus and want to make a difference. They're your brothers and sisters. Whether they look anything like you or not, they're your family. And when a whole generation says, "Go!" you can move mountains.

None of us can do what all of us can do. Remember Jesus' commission to the disciples? "You [all of you collectively] will be my witnesses" (Acts 1:8 NIV).

Jesus didn't issue individual assignments. He didn't move one by one down the line and knight each individual.

"You, Peter, will be by witness . . . "

"You, John, will be my witness . . . "

"You, Mary Magdalene, will be my witness . . . "

But rather, "You (the sum of you) will be my witnesses . . . " Jesus works in community.—ML

This was Jesus' plan all along.

MAX

In fact, working together was so important to Jesus that there are no personal pronouns in the Bible's earliest description of the church in the book of Acts. Not a single one.

No *I* or *me*.

No *he* or *she*.

Just a lot of *theys* and *thems*.

All the believers devoted themselves to the apostles' teaching, and to fellowship, and to sharing in meals (including the Lord's Supper), and to prayer. A deep sense of awe came over them all, and the apostles performed many miraculous signs and wonders. And all the believers met together in one place and shared everything they had. They sold their property and possessions and shared the money with those in need. They worshiped together at the Temple each day, met in homes for the Lord's Supper, and shared their meals with great joy. . . . (Acts 2:42–46 NLT)

See? Only plural nouns and pronouns.
"All the believers."
"Devoted themselves."
"Awe came over them all."
"All the believers met together . . . and shared everything."
"They sold their property and possessions and shared."
"They worshiped together . . . and shared their meals."

We are in this together. In fact, the Bible says we aren't just family. We're all part of the same body—the body of Christ. Check out these two verses:

"We are parts of his body" (Ephesians 5:30).

"He is the head of the body, which is the church" (Colossians 1:18).

We—together—are his body. And we're supposed to get together and act like it.

JENNA

Comparing. Why do we do it? Envy. Why bother? The Bible makes it clear that everyone has a role and specific purpose in changing the world.

"If each part of the body were the same part, there would be no body. But truly God put all the parts, each one of them, in the body as he wanted them" (1 Corinthians 12:18–19).

Yet for some reason, we want to sing like her. Play the guitar like him. Be smart like her. Play basketball like him. We constantly want to be someone else, when God is saying, "No! If you are not you, then the body will be missing a part. The body can't function without YOU."

Isn't that refreshing news? You can rest in being you and knowing that you are essential to the body of Christ. So stop thinking anyone else's role is better than yours. Let's stop comparing ourselves, thinking we don't matter.

Instead, let's listen to the truth:

1 Corinthians 12:22–23: "Those parts of the body that seem to be the weaker are really necessary. And the parts of the body we think are less deserving are the parts to which we give the most honor."

Looks like the goal is to work together here, understanding that God uses us as individual ingredients to mix and make a scrumptious masterpiece.

Whether you are an earlobe, an eyelid, or a kidney, you play an important part in changing the world for him. You may not think an eyelid is as necessary as a heart, but without eyelids, the eyeballs would dry out, get lots of stuff in them, and eventually the body would go blind.

You can change the world in a BIG way when you work together with all the other parts. All your family. In order for the body to function properly, all the parts have to be in top shape—and they have to work together. Unity matters to God. There is "one flock and one shepherd" (John 10:16 NIV).

So what happens if you engage in a family feud? What if you just don't like a brother or sister? What if a Christ-follower you know is annoying, obnoxious, or immature? What if you constantly clash with Miss Bible-Know-It-All or Mr. Pretend-I'm-a-Christian-but-Don't-Really-Act-Like-It?

The body malfunctions.

And if you remember the last time you had the stomach flu, a body that malfunctions isn't pretty.

And it sure isn't making a difference.

The Family Feud pits two families against each other to answer questions. It premiered on ABC in 1976 and is still a popular game show today.

We can't say, "I don't need you" to other Christ-followers, whether they are our best friends, the guy or girl we find annoying, or the stranger from another church or school. The jock needs the chess player. Big youth groups need to work with smaller youth groups. The musicians need the singers. Organized leaders need the creative followers. Cooperating with each other is a command.

What if the whole body were an eye? If you were a collection of eyeballs, how would you function? Five eyes on your hand, which is an eye, attached to your arm-sized eye, affixed to a torso eye, from which extends your neck eye, and . . . The thought is ridiculous! You'd have to bathe in Visine. Then again, you couldn't bathe, because you wouldn't have hands.

The eye cannot say to the hand, "I don't need you!" (1 Corinthians 12:21)—ML

MAX ||||||||||||||||||||||||||||||||||||||||||||||||||||||||||||||||||||||||||||||||||||||||||||||||||||||||||||||||||

"Make every effort to keep the unity of the Spirit through the bond of peace" (Ephesians 4:3 NIV).

Why? Because teamwork can change the world. Jesus said so.

"When two of you get together on anything at all on earth and make a prayer of it, my Father in heaven goes into action. And when two or three of you are together because of me, you can be sure that I'll be there" (Matthew 18:19–20 MSG).

This is an incredible promise. It says that when believers agree, Jesus takes notice, shows up, and hears our prayers. He goes into action.

But if believers argue over which church is better, whether you should use regular bread or those little wafer things for communion, or whether Christian rock music is bad or the best thing since a hot Krispy Kreme doughnut, then we can't accomplish anything.

When workers divide, it is the suffering who suffer the most.

And they've suffered enough, don't you think?

The early church found a way to work together. They found common ground in the death and resurrection of Christ. Because they did, lives were changed. And when you get together with others who believe, you will impact the lives of real people.

People like José Ferreira.

José runs a small pharmacy in a slum of Rio de Janeiro, Brazil. It's really just a shed and bench, but since he sells medicine, it bears the hand-painted sign *Farmácia*. He started his store with three dollars' worth of medical supplies that he bought from a larger pharmacy downtown. As soon as he sells the medicine, he closes his store, walks to a nearby bus stop, rides one hour to the larger pharmacy, and buys more products for his store.

By the time he returns, it is dark, so he waits until the next morning and repeats the cycle: open, sell the product, close the store, and travel to purchase more items for the store. Some days he does this twice. Since his store is closed as much as it is open, he hardly makes a profit. He and his family live in the back of the shack. They stay alive somehow on the equivalent of three dollars a day. If rains wash away his shack, he will lose everything. If one of his children comes down with a tropical fever, he likely will not have the money for medicine. José knows this. But what can he do? He lives in the world of the poor.

But while José is struggling in Rio, God is working in London. A good-hearted taxi driver named Thomas reads an article in a magazine. It is a story about something called *microfinance*.

The prefix "micro-" means "small."

Microfinance provides small loans to poor people so they can increase their income. That way they won't be as vulnerable. Thomas the taxi driver is not rich, but he is blessed. He would happily help a fellow businessperson on the other side of the world. But how can he? Can a British taxi driver help a Brazilian merchant? Through organizations that help microfinance, he can.

So he does.

A few days later José is offered a microloan of fifty-five dollars. He and six other neighbors in his community get loans. They must all guarantee each other's loans. That means that if one of the six people does not pay the money back, the other five will be responsible for it. If José does not repay the loan, his friends will have to cover for him. Since the men are friends, no one will want to let his friends down. That kind of positive peer pressure helps keep microfinance programs successful.

Fifty-five dollars is just eleven friends or neighbors each chipping in five bucks, less than the price of a movie ticket.

José puts the loan to good use. With the extra money, he is able to stop making daily trips for more supplies. He can keep his store open all day. After two years of growing his business and paying back his loans, he saves a thousand dollars, buys his own piece of land, and is collecting concrete cinder blocks for a house.

In 2006, the Nobel Peace Prize was awarded to Muhammad Yunus, a founder of the microfinance movement.

Who did God use to help José Ferreira? A taxi driver. A humanitarian organization. His own friends and neighbors. They all worked together. Isn't it cool how God uses different parts of his body to change lives?

This is how he worked in Jerusalem. No one can do everything, but everyone can do something. And when we do, BIG things happen. BIG differences are made. When the church in Acts did it, everyone had what they needed. Don't we want that for our world?

The apostles testified powerfully to the resurrection of the Lord Jesus, and God's great blessing was upon them all. There were no needy people among them.
(Acts 4:33–34 NLT, emphasis added)

HOPE International is a Christian microfinance organization that helps people around the world. You can join in by taking a photograph of your hand with a word written on it that you think describes people who are growing businesses because of microloans. For example, you might write the word "Hope." Upload the picture to the HOPE Hands photo album on Shutterfly, and $5 will be donated to finance microloans for entrepreneurs in need. Visit *hopehandsup.shutterfly.com*.

When you and your friends get together, BIG things can happen. That's what fourteen-year-old Jordan Baker discovered when he got together with friends.

JORDAN'S STORY

When Jordan Baker was ten years old, he learned he could make a difference. His dad, a law enforcement lieutenant, was helping with a campaign to get the sheriff reelected. Jordan walked in parades and helped put up signs. He discovered what it felt like to get involved in something bigger than he could accomplish by himself.

Once he became a teenager, Jordan wanted to do something on his own.

Jordan Baker leads a CCTA meeting

When his mom learned that there was no one to organize the National Day of Prayer in Brooksville, Florida, Jordan helped her plan it. Within eight days, they pulled an event together that involved fifteen dignitaries and twelve churches. Plus, Jordan got a group of his friends to come and speak about the Founding Fathers. That sparked the idea for Conservative Christian Teens for America, a club founded by Jordan that invites middle and high schoolers to make a difference in their communities and across the nation. He wants Christians ages ten to seventeen to learn about the Christian roots America has, to study the words of the Founding Fathers, and to reclaim America's Christian heritage. In just a few short months, the group grew from Jordan, his younger brother, and a couple of friends to more than fifty teens.

continued »

CCTA members with the pillowcases they made for kids with cancer

Now CCTA meets on a weekly basis and helps wherever it is needed. In its first six months, CCTA did a neighborhood cleanup, walked in a local veterans' parade, and made six-hundred pillowcases for children with cancer. The group also practices public speaking and is learning American history from a Christian perspective.

It's not always easy to study documents like the Constitution or the Federalist Papers, to show up at volunteer events on their free time, or to write and give speeches to peers. But CCTA members say it's worth the hard work.

"This is our rebellion against low expectations," CCTA member Olivia Terlep told us. "It may be hard, but sometimes hard means it's the right thing to do."

ConKerr Cancer provides colorful, fun pillowcases to children with cancer to brighten their hospital stays. ConKerr volunteers also visit cancer patients and bring materials to help kids sew their own pillowcases, giving them a distraction from their illness and a feeling of accomplishment. To find out how you can help, visit ConKerrcancer.org.

Once you get some friends together, what should you do?

➡ Choose a meeting place (a church, your school, your home) and time (weekly, every other week, nights, weekends).

➡ Ask one or more adults to be your group's sponsor and to help you troubleshoot your projects.

➡ Open and close every meeting with prayer. Ask God to show up and guide you in the right direction. Read the Bible too. Learning more about God together is important because it makes your faith stronger. The Bible says it's like iron sharpening iron (Proverbs 27:17).

➡ At the first meeting, introduce yourself and share your desire to make a difference. Invite others to share why they came.

➡ Brainstorm ideas that your group can do.

➡ If you have a specific project you want the group to accomplish, do your homework first. Find out what types of services or items are needed. Make sure you anticipate whether you can handle it. Can you raise the funds, get enough volunteers, and work together without clashing?

➡ Start simple. If you choose too large of a project your first time, you might get discouraged and give up.

. . . .

As you start thinking about college, consider attending a Christian university or taking the summer after graduation or a year off to go on a foreign mission trip. That may seem like a long time from now, but it's never too early to start working toward your goals. And learning more about God's world and seeing his people in different places can help you make a difference that will outlive your life.

. . . .

→ Combine resources. Make a list of the unique talents and training each group member has. Also, find out what you can each give in terms of money, time, merchandise, food, or service.

→ When planning an event, picture the event as if you were a guest from the moment you walk in the door until you leave. Are there signs telling you how to get there? Are you greeted at the door by a volunteer? Are there tickets? Who is collecting the money? If food is served, will you eat standing up or at a table? Will you need trash cans? Recycle bins? No item is too small to consider.

→ Extend grace and mercy. Accept each other's differences. Some people are always running late. Some are complainers. Others want to run the show. It takes the whole body to do what God wants us to do. Look past the faults and see each unique person God has brought to your group.

School group projects. Can it get any worse? There are always two stereotypical extremes:

→ The student who ends up taking on all the work, not relying on the group.

→ The student who doesn't do anything, depending on the group too much.

Which extreme was I?

If you guessed that I was the gal who couldn't trust the

group, you're right. The goody-goody, straight-A student who couldn't afford a slacker who might mess up her GPA. And it killed me! Not only would I give up every second of sleep to do the project, but also I prevented the rest of the group from using their abilities. I was enabling laziness due to my lack of trust and control-freakishness. (I know; I just made up that word.)

When we are on the same team, sure, we may not always make a perfect A-plus, but we learn to lean on one another, rejoice with one another, challenge one another. And isn't that worth more than a temporary grade?

～～～～～～～～～～～～～～～～～～～

If you work together, you can set up a lemonade stand or hold a car wash. If you join forces with others, you can teach Vacation Bible School to kids in your neighborhood or start a worship band. You can clean a new mom's house or help take dinners to a family in need. And the more you do, the bigger the impact. The bigger the impact, the more people will notice. The more people notice, the more believers will want to join in, and those who don't know Christ might come to meet him. The more people who join in, the more help will reach those in need.

If your group wants to hold a car wash, check with a local auto parts store. Some chains allow groups to hold car washes at their stores and provide the hoses, buckets, soap, and scrubbing tools for you!

Effort by effort, the world changes. It's exciting to watch, but nothing beats being part of it. It's a grand adventure, led by God himself.

With every cup of lemonade consumed,
people are helped.

With every commitment to Christ,
a life is spared.

With every part of the body doing its job,
God is glorified.

That's what real family looks like.

Two are better than one, because they have a good return for their work: If one falls down, his friend can help him up. But pity the man who falls and has no one to help him up!

Ecclesiastes 4:9–10 NIV

Lord, what an amazing opportunity you have spread out before me—a chance to make a difference for you in a desperately hurting world. Help me to see the needs you want me to see, to react in a way that honors you, and to bless others. Help me to work with others as a team and to worship as a team. Give me the strength to partner with you and with my brothers and sisters in Christ to meet the needs you place before us. Help me fulfill your plan for me in my own generation.

In Jesus' name I pray, amen.

CHAPTER 10

HANG OUT YOUR WELCOME SIGN

They ate together in their homes, happy to share their food with joyful hearts.

Acts 2:46

JENNA

Have you noticed? We now substitute "text" where we used to say "talk."

> "I talked to that guy last night" = "I texted that guy last night."

No wonder we have so much drama these days! Talk about communication breakdown! When we text, we can't hear the person's tone, see his eyes, notice her smile, so we are left to wonder . . .

"Is she mad at me?"

"What do you think he meant by that?"

"Do you think he was joking?"

On top of communication breakdown, we are having physical breakdowns. Just ask Annie Levitz, a teen I just read about who was diagnosed with carpal tunnel syndrome, a nerve problem that causes a lot of pain in the hand/wrist area. How did she get carpal tunnel? From texting. No, I'm not kidding.[1]

But probably the scariest side-effect of texting is the confidence breakdown. A lot of guys aren't walking up to girls to ask them out anymore. They are hiding behind a safe keypad. I'm guilty too. Whenever I have to back out of something, it's a lot easier for me to shoot off a text saying, "Sorry, I can't make it," instead of calling and admitting that I'm bailing out.

We are arguing, confessing, sharing personal experiences . . . all behind a keypad. You know what this does to us? It makes us uncomfortable with real confrontation. It also makes us less personal. We rely on words on a screen to share our hearts instead of using the eyes, mouth, and ears God gave us to interact, communicate, and love on people.

Am I saying texting is bad? NO! I love to text! But is it taking us away from true, heart-to-heart, sharing-life, personal relationships? Maybe . . .

~~~~~~~~~~~~~~~~~~~~~~~~~~~~~~~~~~~~~

Once upon a time, in a land not so far away, there were no texts or tweets, no social media sites or voice-activated routing programs. You couldn't send money via PayPal or order anything online. You had to have real money, and to get it you had to go to the bank and visit a teller. Real, live phone operators put you on hold. And in some ways, we were better off for it.

MAX ||||||||||||||||||||||||||||||||||||||||||||||||||||||||||||||||||||||||||||||||||||||||||||

Call us a fast culture, a tech-savvy culture, but don't call us a personal culture. Our society is set up for isolation. We wear earbuds when we do our homework, watch DVDs to pass the time at home, and listen to our iPods in the car. We communicate via e-mail and text messages. We even go in and out of our houses with gate and garage-door openers, rarely hanging outside to say hi to the neighbors.

The theme seems to be: "I leave you alone. You leave me alone."

Yet God wants his people to be an exception. Let everyone else sit only in front of screens and keyboards. God's children will be people who open their doors and open their hearts.

Long before the first Christians had church buildings or special places to baptize people, they had kitchens and dinner tables. "The believers met together in the Temple every day. They ate together *in their homes*, happy to share their food with joyful hearts" (Acts 2:46, emphasis added). "Every day in the Temple and *in people's homes* they continued teaching the people and telling the Good News—that Jesus is the Christ" (Acts 5:42, emphasis added).

Kitchens and living rooms show up all over the New Testament. People's homes were the gathering place of the church. "To Philemon our beloved friend and fellow laborer . . . and to the church in your house" (Philemon vv. 1–2 NKJV). "Greet Priscilla and Aquila . . . the church that is in their house" (Romans 16:3, 5 NKJV). "Greet the brethren who are in Laodicea, and Nymphas and the church that is in his house" (Colossians 4:15 NKJV).

Get the picture?

It's time to come out of your room and into the *living* room. To put away the iPod and talk to people. To eat and laugh and love God together. To turn off the TV and open your doors wide to make other people feel at home with you.

Consider how brilliantly God did it in the early church. The first generation of Christians was made up of a lot of cultures and backgrounds. At least fifteen different nationalities heard Peter's sermon on the Day of Pentecost. Jews stood next to Gentiles. Men worshiped with women. Slaves and masters both sought after Christ. Can people of such different backgrounds and cultures get along with each other?

We wonder the same thing today. Can blacks live in peace with whites? Can football players find common ground with techies? Can a Christian family carry on a civil friendship with the Muslim family down the street? Can seriously different people get along?

The early church did

through the clearest of messages

(the Cross)

and the simplest of tools

(the home).

Not everyone can go serve God in a foreign country, start a huge hunger relief organization, or volunteer at the downtown soup kitchen. But everyone can offer some kind of hospitality.

Do you have a front door, a seat in the lunchroom, a living

room or family room? A table? Chairs? Bread and meat, or even peanut butter and jelly for sandwiches? Great! You just qualified to serve in the most ancient of ministries: hospitality. You can join the ranks of people such as . . .

Abraham. He fed, not just angels,
but the Lord of angels (see Genesis 18).

Rahab. She received and protected the spies. Thanks to her kindness, her family survived, and her name is remembered (see Joshua 6:22–23; Matthew 1:5).

Martha and Mary. They opened their home for Jesus. He, in turn, raised their brother Lazarus from the dead (see John 11:1–45; Luke 10:38–42).

Zacchaeus. He welcomed Jesus to his table. And Jesus left salvation as a thank-you gift (see Luke 19:1–10).

And what about the greatest example of all—the guy known only as the "certain man" in Matthew 26:18? On the day before his death, Jesus told his followers, "Go into the city to a certain man and tell him, 'The Teacher says: The chosen time is near. I will have the Passover with my followers at your house.'" The man opened his house, and the Savior came and dined there with his disciples. How cool is that!

How would you have liked to be the one who opened his home for Jesus? You know what? You still can be. Remember: "Whatever you did for one of the least of these brothers of mine, you did for me" (Matthew 25:40 NIV).

When you welcome people you don't know very well to your table, people different from you, people who have needs you can fill, you are welcoming God himself. Something happens around a dinner table that will never happen in a sanctuary. In a church auditorium you see the backs of heads. Around the table you see the expressions on faces. In the auditorium one person speaks; around the table everyone has a voice. Church services begin and end at certain times. Around the table there is time to talk.

> It's no accident that hospitality and hospital come from the same Latin word, for they both accomplish the same thing: healing.

When you open your door to someone, you are sending this message: "You matter to me and to God." You may think you are saying, "Come over for a visit." But what your guest hears is, "I'm worth the effort."

> I expect to pass through this life but once. If therefore, there be any kindness I can show, or any good thing I can do to any fellow being, let me do it now, and not defer or neglect it, as I shall not pass this way again.
>
> —William Penn, founder of Pennsylvania

How can you show hospitality to these people? Maybe your parents aren't wild about you bringing a lot of company home. But would they let you have friends over once a week or even a couple of times a month to eat and learn more about God? Could you bake some brownies or cookies and invite people to share your table and your goodies? Would you be the one to volunteer to show the new student around school? Or maybe your hospitality can hit the road, as you take a meal or some muffins to an older person, a sick person, or someone who has trouble getting out of the house.

What ways can you think of to welcome people into your life? How can you show hospitality?

1. ....

2. ....

3. ....

4. ....

Can you believe that some people pass an entire day without one meaningful contact with anyone else? Think how lonely that must be!

Some residents who live in nursing homes or assisted living facilities never have a visitor. You can share hospitality by getting permission to visit a home. Find out if you can bring some homemade cookies or food. Play a game of checkers, let an older person share memories with you, or sing some songs together.

MAX ⁞⁞⁞

Your hospitality can be a lonely person's hospital. Here's where to start.

Give them an invitation. First, work out with your parents a good time for your guests to come. Then let your guests know you want them to come. Call them on the phone, or stop by their house. Make your invitation personal. Don't send it by e-mail, text, or instant message. Say something as simple as, "I'd love for us to hang out tonight. Come over and eat with us." The person you invite may have just had a terrible day—feeling rejected at school, being teased, or dumped by a crush. Your invitation says, "I want to spend time with you!"

Such a little thing can change a life.

Make a big deal out of their arrival. Be waiting at the front door. Make a welcome sign or poster, or tie some balloons on the mailbox or door. Make it feel like a party in their honor. If you have a driveway, go outside and meet them before they get to the door. If your apartment has a lobby, be waiting for them. This is a great event. One of God's children is coming to your house!

Make sure you get your guests what they need. If you were a member of the first church, you'd be washing dirty feet whenever someone came over. You're off the hook on that one today, but you should have food and drink ready. And you should try not to be rushed or look bored. Take time to talk and listen. Turn off radios and televisions that might distract you. Don't text or answer your cell phone when someone's talking. In fact, turn off the phone. Get unplugged.

Go around the table and share the best and worst parts of your day or week. When we share our table and share our lives, we restore souls.

Love to work with kids? Want to extend your hospitality to kids in your city? Child Evangelism Fellowship wants every child to hear the gospel, and its Christian Youth in Action camps train teens like you to teach children about God. The one-to two-week camps show you how to present the gospel on a child's level and then lead a kids' club ministry in your community or neighborhood. Depending on the state you serve in, you might teach clubs from one to five weeks during the summer. Visit CEFonline.com and search "CYIA" for more information.

If you just can't open your home to friends, remember that hospitality can happen outside your home too. So invite someone you want to encourage to a picnic or bring a snack to share at school.

Let people know you really care about what's happening in their lives.

Here are some fun icebreakers to get people talking:

➜ Ask questions like: "If we could invite a famous person from history to be here with us, who would you invite? What questions would you ask that person?"

continued »

> ➡ Have people in the group tell about their favorite books, movies, foods, or activities.
>
> ➡ Read the news for unusual or unique, fun articles. Use these topics to start a story, and ask questions that can't be answered with just a yes or a no.

Send people home with a blessing. Make sure your guests know you are glad they came. If you can afford one, give them a small party favor or gift. Or write thank-you notes ahead of time and give the notes to your company as they leave, thanking them for coming and giving them words of encouragement.

> The Meals on Wheels Association of America has been delivering hot meals and providing places where people can come together for a hot meal since 1976. MOWAA volunteers can help make meals or pick up boxed hot meals daily to deliver to those who have trouble leaving their homes, such as the elderly and handicapped. Maybe your family would like to deliver meals, or you can get a group of friends to find out what foods MOWAA needs to have donated and collect them. To find out about Meals on Wheels in your area, visit MOWAA.org.

Another thing about hospitality is this: don't wait for the perfect time, place, and party favors. It doesn't have to be fancy to touch the heart. Your house doesn't have to be big. Your dishes don't all have to match. You don't have to serve a gourmet meal. Chips and dip, a bowl of M&Ms, or a five-dollar pizza will do just fine.

Just make sure there's a roll of toilet paper in the bathroom, comfortable places to sit, and enough real smiles to make everyone loosen up. Because if we wait until everything is perfect, we'll never invite anyone over.

Nothing says hospitality like homemade chocolate-chip cookies. Here's a recipe so you can spread the love. Yum!

Ingredients:

2 ¼ cups all-purpose flour
1 teaspoon baking soda
1 teaspoon salt
1 cup (2 sticks) butter, softened
3/4 cup granulated sugar
3/4 cup packed brown sugar
1 teaspoon vanilla extract
2 large eggs
2 cups (12-oz. pkg.) chocolate chips

Directions:

Preheat oven to 375° F. Combine flour, baking soda, and salt in small bowl. Beat butter, granulated sugar, brown sugar, and vanilla extract in large mixer bowl until creamy. Add eggs, one at a time, beating well after each addition. Gradually beat in flour mixture. Stir in chocolate chips. Drop by rounded tablespoon onto ungreased baking sheets. Bake for 9 to 11 minutes or until golden brown.

Remember this: what is ordinary to you is a banquet to someone else. You think your house is small, but to the lonely heart, it is a castle.

You think the living room is a mess with your little sister's toys all over it, but to the person whose life is a mess, your house is a safe place.

You think the meal is simple, but to those who eat alone every night, pork and beans and hot dogs on paper plates taste as good as a juicy steak and loaded potato.

What is small to you is huge to them.—ML

When you begin your journey of hospitality, look beyond your circle of friends. Be certain to invite those who need you most. Jesus said, "When you give a banquet, invite the poor, the crippled, the lame, the blind, and you will be blessed" (Luke 14:13–14 NIV). Maybe you don't know anyone with a physical disability like Jesus describes, but you know kids who are the outcasts, the misfits. You may know some friends who don't have as much as you do. You may have visitors to your youth group who don't have any Christians in their family. The point is this: Don't be afraid to reach out to someone new.

Never be afraid to do something new.
Remember, the amateur Noah built the ark;
professionals built the Titanic.

—Anonymous

MAX

The Greek word for *hospitality* is made up of two terms that translate *love* and *stranger*. The word literally means "to love a stranger." Everyone can welcome a guest we know and love. But can we welcome someone we don't know well? Every morning in America more than 39 million people wake up in poverty.[2] In 2008, 17 million households had difficulty providing food for their families.[3] An estimated 1.1 million children lived in households experiencing hunger multiple times throughout the year.[4] And this is in America, the wealthiest nation in the history of the world.

When the government gives the poor food stamps, their bodies won't starve from hunger. But food stamps can't fill up hearts and souls. When we invite people to our own table, we make them feel like they have value. We help them feel good about themselves! Who would have thought? God's secret weapons in the war on poverty include inviting someone to share dinner with you and your family.

A few months ago, I (Max) was sitting at the red light of a busy intersection when I noticed a man walking toward my car. He stepped off the curb, bypassed several vehicles, and started waving at me. He carried a cardboard sign under his arm, a jammed pack on his back. His jeans were baggy, his beard was scraggly, and he was calling my name. "Max! Max! Remember me?"

I lowered my window. He smiled a toothless grin. "I still remember that burger you bought me." Then I remembered. Months, maybe a year earlier, at this very intersection, I had taken him to a corner hamburger stand where we enjoyed a meal together. He was California-bound on that day. "I'm passing through Texas again," he told me. The light changed, and cars began to honk. I pulled away, leaving him waving and shouting, "Thanks for the burger, Max."

You never know what one meal will do.

One time after Jesus rose from the dead, he starts walking next to two of the disciples as they walk from Jerusalem to their village. The trail is a seven-mile journey, which took a large part of the day, even for grown, healthy men. They talk the entire time. Jesus talks about the Bible, beginning with the teachings of Moses right up to the events of their day. But get this: the whole time, the disciples don't recognize him.

As they get near their village, Jesus acts like he's going to keep walking. The disciples had another idea. "But they urged him strongly, 'Stay with us, for it is nearly evening; the day is almost over'" (Luke 24:29 NIV).

It had been a long day for the disciples. But their fellow traveler touched their hearts, made them think. So they welcomed him in. They pulled out an extra chair, poured some water in the soup, and offered bread. Jesus blessed the bread, and when he did, "their eyes were opened and they recognized him" (v. 31 NIV).

We still encounter people on the road of life. And sometimes we feel a connection, affection. We want to spend time with them, invite them to be part of our lives. As much as you can, extend the invitation. You never know who you might be inviting to dinner.

Cheerfully share your home with those who need a meal or a place to stay. God has given each of you a gift from his great variety of spiritual gifts. Use them well to serve one another.

1 Peter 4:9–10 NLT

God, thank you for giving me so much. Thank you for the things that I take for granted—a bed, a roof over my head, even air to breathe! God, I pray that you would help me take these blessings and share them with other people. It's really easy for me to stay closed off. Open my heart to be more inviting and hospitable. Give me the courage to talk to others in a world that lives behind keypads. Give me the boldness to invite strangers over in a world where we are comfortable in our own little communities. Help me to break down barriers and touch people's hearts with your love.

In Jesus' name I pray, amen.

CHAPTER 11

BLAST THE WALLS DOWN

Christ accepted you, so you should accept each other, which will bring glory to God.

—Romans 15:7

We want to take you to a football game.

Yes, now. Get ready to cheer on your favorite team.

Oops, wait a minute.

Both teams are your favorite tonight . . . if you are from Faith Christian High School.

MAX

Because at one particular Faith Christian football game, there was a very odd sight. Fans of the proud, Grapevine, Texas, team rooted for the opposition. Cheerleaders cheered for the other guys. Parents yelled for the competition—by name!

What in the world? Was it Backwards Day?

No. Just a big-hearted football coaching staff and seventy dedicated high school football players acting like spiritual dynamite, blasting down the walls around some very crusty hearts. They wanted to make a difference. They practiced hospitality. And they learned how good it feels to partner with God in the process.

Here's what happened. Coach Kris Hogan got the idea that when his team was going to play Gainesville State, Faith should make them feel welcome. After all, Faith Christian definitely had the advantage. Great equipment, dedicated players, and parents who care. Faith's fans and family members make banners, attend pep rallies, and wouldn't miss a game for their own funeral. Gainesville's players, on the other hand, wear seven-year-old shoulder pads and last decade's helmets and show up at each game wearing handcuffs. Their parents don't watch them play, but twelve uniformed officers do.

That's because Gainesville is a maximum-security correctional facility. The school doesn't have a stadium, cheerleading squad, or half a hope of winning. Gainesville was 0–8 going into the Grapevine game. They'd scored two touchdowns all year. Faith Christian was 7–2.

The whole situation didn't seem fair. So Coach Hogan devised a plan. He asked the fans to step across the field and cheer for the other side. More than two hundred volunteered.

They formed a forty-yard spirit line. They painted "Go Tornadoes!" on a banner that the Gainesville squad could burst through. They sat on the Gainesville side of the stadium. They even learned the roster of Gainesville players so they could yell for the players by name.

The prisoners had heard people scream at them before, but never like this. Gerald, a lineman who will serve three years, said, "People are a little afraid of us when we come to

the games. You can see it in their eyes. They're lookin' at us
like we're criminals. But these people, they were yellin' for us.
By our names!"

After the game the teams gathered in the middle of the
field to say a prayer. One of the Gainesville players, Isaiah,
asked to lead it. Coach Hogan agreed, not knowing what to
expect. "Lord," the boy said, "I don't know how this happened,
so I don't know how to say thank you, but I never would've
known there was so many people in the world that
cared about us."

Grapevine fans weren't finished. After the game,
they waited beside the Gainesville bus to give each
player a good-bye gift—burger, fries, candy, soda, a Bible, an
encouraging letter, and a round of applause. As their prison
bus left the parking lot, the players pressed stunned faces
against the windows and wondered what had just hit them.[1]

Here's what hit them: a platoon of prejudice-demolition
experts.

Their assignment? Blast preconceived notions into dust.

Their weapons? Actions that showed "You still matter"
and "Someone still cares."

Their mission? Break down the barricades that separate
God's children from each other.

And they succeeded. They were dynamite to the walls and
kryptonite to the enemy. They were part of God's grand adventure. Don't you think that felt great?

What walls divide your world? There you stand on one
side. And on the other? The classmate you just can't stand.
The guy with the cigarettes and tattoos. The rich kid who is
always bragging about his newest video game or toy. The person on the opposite side of your beliefs. The homeless man
who stands at the red light near your church every week.

The first church knew about walls. They built real walls to keep enemies from attacking, but don't you think walls also shut the unwanted out? Like the Samaritans outside Jerusalem.

Talk about a wall. "Jews," as John wrote in his gospel, "refuse to have anything to do with Samaritans" (John 4:9 NLT). The two cultures had hated each other for a thousand years. Samaritans were blacklisted. Their beds, utensils—even their spit—were considered unclean.[2] No orthodox Jew would travel into the region. Most Jews would gladly go twice as far to avoid going through Samaria.

Jesus, however, played by a different set of rules. He spent the better part of a day with a Samaritan woman—on her turf—drinking water from her ladle, discussing her questions (John 4:1–26). Jesus loves to break down walls.

"Christ brought us together through his death on the cross. The Cross got us to embrace, and that was the end of the hostility" (Ephesians 2:16 MSG).

Do you need to ask Jesus to forgive you for building walls against any one person or group of people in particular? If so, you might say something like this:

Father, I'm sorry for holding grudges and judging others. Because you care about them, help me care about them. Help me to see past my prejudice and into their hearts. And would you help them forgive me, as well? I love you, Lord. Thanks for loving my messed-up heart. Help me to love other messed-up hearts because of the Cross.

Alex and Brett Harris are knocking down the cultural walls of low expectations for teens. The twin brothers founded a blog called The Rebelution when they were sixteen to encourage teens to start using their talents and time for Jesus right now. To be the dynamite that blasts down walls.

ALEX AND BRETT'S STORY

Alex and Brett Harris grew up with five brothers and sisters in a homeschooling family. Their dad helped get the homeschooling movement started and became known for speaking and writing books. Their older brother, Joshua, became an author at twenty-one when he wrote a book called *I Kissed Dating Goodbye*. The twins grew up learning about Jesus, and because of what they saw their dad and brother accomplish, they knew God could use anyone.

Alex Harris speaking at a Rebelution Tour conference

"My dad didn't graduate from high school; he ran away from home when he was fifteen," Alex told us.[3] "Yet we have gotten to see God use him powerfully in a number of ways in the homeschool community. Then our older brother Josh wrote a best-selling book. I know that growing up in the shadow of people who are so well known could be very smothering, but I think for Brett and me it just made us realize

continued »

that God can use normal guys like our big brother and our dad. You may think God uses superstars who have never sinned or only amazing people, but no. God uses your big brother and your dad and you. Normal, ordinary you."

When the twins were sixteen, their dad gave them a list of books to read over the summer. There were Christian classics and business books, hard books that required them to get out of their comfort zone. They realized that many teens are wasting too much of their time, looking for a purpose, killing time on the Internet or at the movies, not really giving to anyone else. But they knew plenty of kids who wanted to make a difference. So they started a blog called The Rebelution. The official definition of the "rebelution" is "a teenage rebellion against low expectations." It's a combination of the words *rebellion* and *revolution*.

"But in this case, it's not a rebellion against God-established authority, but against the low expectations of our society. It's a refusal to be defined by our ungodly, rebellious, and apathetic culture. Actually, we like to think of it as rebelling against rebellion," TheRebelution.com site says. Soon, the blog became a hugely popular teen online community and attracted media attention. The brothers were interviewed in *USA Today* and other news outlets. Then they got an offer to prove they meant what they said. An Alabama Supreme Court Justice asked the brothers to serve as his interns for a semester. At sixteen, they were the youngest interns to walk the halls. They worked a lot, learned a lot, and showed that young people can work as hard—or even harder—than adults. They made such an impression that they went on to direct the justice's reelection campaign, recruiting teens from around the country to man phone banks, hand out flyers, and even schedule media interviews.

At age eighteen, the twins turned their experiences into a book for teens called *Do Hard Things*. They followed it up with another book, *Start Here*.[4] They talk to teens all over the country at their *Do Hard Things* and *Start Here* conferences, getting their peers fired up to throw off their laziness and get explosive for God.

"I don't think a young person has to have a vision from God or already know their very specific calling; a lot of times it's just being faithful with what God has given you and then not being afraid when God opens the door for a bigger opportunity," Alex says. "The Rebelution started as a very small conviction that our generation was being sold a lie about what the teen years were about. *Do Hard Things* is about breaking the stereotype that teens are apathetic and lazy.

"We really can be faithful and hardworking and competent, even as young people. We start by being faithful in the little things, then believe that God can use us in amazing ways to do something that is beyond us."

Alex says he and Brett certainly experienced the truth that there is power in numbers. Once teens got talking, whole movements started.

continued »

Brett Harris speaking at a Rebelution Tour conference

"We felt like we were just riding the rocket and have been for the last couple of years," he says. "It's been incredible to see how young people everywhere have the potential to make a difference as they, first of all, fall in love with Jesus and believe he is faithful. Then they are able to do the impossible.

"We've seen teens like Joshua Guthrie, who started Dollar for a Drink, and has now raised forty thousand dollars to dig four wells in the Sudan. But just as involved are the young people doing small things, like scraping ice off an older lady's windshield when they saw her struggling in a parking lot. Or the young men we know who felt led to step outside their comfort zone in a big way and lead their youth group when their leader had to be away on medical leave. When they challenged their peers to live for God, they realized for the first time how God could use them. Now they know they have a heart for young people or children's ministry. That one decision to help set their lives on a totally different direction. They now have a clear sense of how God wants to use them."

Check out The Rebelution blog at TheRebelution.com.

Alex and Brett—and thousands and thousands of "rebelutionaries"—are changing the world one act of kindness at a time. One act of faithfulness at a time. One sacrifice of their own time or money at a time. They are true dynamite. Because, like the kids at Faith Christian and Gainesville State learned, when you cross the field to cheer for the other side, everyone wins.

During the first days of the church, a man named Ananias was that kind of dynamite, and every Christian's life from that time forward has been impacted. All because Ananias let God use him. The Lord told him in a vision that he was to go to a man named Saul, because Saul had become a follower of Christ. He had also become blind, and Ananias was to help him.

MAX

Ananias wonders if he misheard the instructions. Wonders if he should turn around and tell his wife where he's going in case he never returns. Because everyone knows Saul. He kills Christians. Ananias doesn't want to die, but he knows he needs to obey.

Arise and go to the street called Straight, and inquire at the house of Judas for one called Saul of Tarsus, for behold, he is praying. And in a vision he has seen a man named Ananias coming in and putting his hand on him, so that he might receive his sight.
(Acts 9:11–12 NKJV)

Ananias scampers through the courtyard of chickens, towering camels, and little donkeys. He steps past the shop of the tailor and doesn't respond to the greeting of the tanner. He keeps moving until he reaches the street called Straight. The inn has low arches and large rooms with mattresses.

Ananias can't turn back now. He ascends the stone stairs. The guards step aside, and Ananias steps into the doorway. He gasps at what he sees. A gaunt man sitting cross-legged on the floor, half shadowed by a shaft of sunlight. Hollow-cheeked and dry-lipped, he rocks back and forth, groaning a prayer. Not the threatening man he had been expecting.

"How long has he been like this?"

"Three days."

Ananias hesitates. If this is a setup, he is history. If not, this moment is making history.

No one could fault Ananias for being worried. When Jewish leaders needed a hit man to terrorize the church, Saul stepped forward. He became the Angel of Death. He descended on the Christians in a fury "uttering threats with every breath" (Acts 9:1 NLT). He "persecuted the church of God beyond measure and tried to destroy it" (Galatians 1:13 NKJV).

But on the road to Damascus, Saul had an encounter with the Lord. He was blinded by it, and he suddenly knew how wrong he had been. Jesus was real. His followers were right. By the time Ananias arrives, blind Saul has begun to see Jesus in a different light.

Ananias sits on the stone floor and says, "Brother Saul, the Lord Jesus, who appeared to you on the road as you came, has sent me that you may receive your sight and be filled with the Holy Spirit" (Acts 9:17 NKJV).

Tears rush like a tide against the crusts on Saul's eyes. The scaly covering loosens and falls away. He blinks and sees the face of his new friend. He gets baptized and starts preaching in a synagogue. The first of a thousand sermons.

Saul soon becomes Paul, and Paul preaches from the hills of Athens, writes letters that become most of the New Testament books, and makes an impact on future Christian writers, preachers, and revolutionaries like St. Thomas Aquinas, Martin Luther, and John Calvin.

God used Paul to touch the world.

But first he used Ananias to touch Paul.

Has God given you a similar assignment? Has God given you a Saul? Someone that everyone else has written off, but you know this person can do great things for God if his life turns around?

No one gives "your Saul" a prayer. But you are beginning to realize that maybe God is at work behind the scenes. Maybe it's too soon to throw in the towel. . . . You begin to believe. Don't resist these thoughts.

Joseph didn't. His brothers sold him into Egyptian slavery. Yet he welcomed them into his palace.

David didn't. King Saul had a vendetta against David, but David had a soft spot for Saul. He called him "the LORD's anointed" (1 Samuel 24:10 NKJV).

You can be the difference for the world. You can be the difference for a Saul. After all, no one believed in people more than Jesus did. He saw something in Peter worth developing, in the thief on the cross worth saving. He believed in Saul. So don't give up on your Saul. When others write him off, give him another chance. Stay strong. Call him brother. Call her sister. Tell your Saul about Jesus, and pray. And remember this: God never sends you where he hasn't already been. By the time you reach your Saul, who knows what you'll find?

Pray every day for thirty days for someone you love who needs to meet Jesus. After thirty days, it should be a habit. Keep praying!

JENNA

Well, she's done it all. Partied, smoked pot, done harder drugs, slept around. . . . Her lifestyle may not look like mine. Her beliefs definitely don't look like mine, but I love her. And I will never give up on her. Slowly but surely, God is using me to show her the faithfulness, love, and gentleness of Jesus. The church she knows would point a nose up and a finger straight at all of her mistakes. But over the years she has noticed that I will listen to it all and still be there.

My persistence prevailed after three years of friendship.

I was the first person she called after a tragic night our freshman year of college. We were literally oceans apart, at separate schools. So when she called, it surprised me. That night she had suffered serious physical abuse from a guy (and some of his friends) she had met at a club. Crying on the other end of the line, she said she didn't know why she called me, but my name was the first to pop into her head.

We prayed together.

I even got to share my favorite scripture.

To this day, we stay in touch. We talk about life and God. The partying and men are still in her life. But God has showed me that only he can completely transform a heart. I'm just called to love her through everything, tell her about the hope of Jesus, and pray that transformation comes.

Will you take a minute and pray for my friend?

Will you take the time, maybe even years, to be a friend to someone like my friend?

Thanks. You never know whose life will be changed.

My favorite Ananias-type story involves a couple of college roommates. The Ananias of the pair was a guy. He put up with his friend's late-night drunkenness, midnight throw-ups, and all day sleep-ins. He didn't complain when his friend disappeared for the weekend or smoked cigarettes in the car. He could have requested a roommate who went to church more or cursed less or cared about something other than impressing girls.

But he hung with his personal Saul, seeming to think that something good could happen if the guy could pull his life together. So he kept cleaning up the mess, inviting his roommate to church, and looking out for him.

I don't remember the Lord coming to me in a bright light or a loud voice. I've never traveled a desert road to Damascus. But I distinctly remember Jesus knocking me off my perch and flipping on the light. It took four semesters, but Steve's example and Jesus' message finally got through. So if this book has inspired you at all, if you're ready to run now, ready to get started making a difference, you might thank God for my Ananias, Steve Green.

I was given mercy so that in me, the worst of all sinners, Christ Jesus could show that he has patience without limit. His patience with me made me an example for those who would believe in him and have life forever.

I Timothy 1:16

Lord, I judge people a lot. I have a hard time loving certain people I think don't deserve your love. But you tell us that NONE of us deserves your love. You tell us we ALL fall short and have messed up. Would you help me see my own messiness? Would you help me see how much I don't deserve you? That's the only way I'll be able to love the others I judge. Give me your eyes to see past the outside and into the heart. And give me your heart to love people where they are in life. Would you show me the ones I need to love more? Thank you for sending Jesus, so that my mistakes wouldn't get in the way my relationship with you. I love you.

In Jesus' name I pray, amen.

CHAPTER 12

HOW TO MAKE A DIFFERENCE EVERY DAY

> I have fought the good fight, I have finished the race, I have kept the faith.
>
> 2 Timothy 4:7

You're ready to get started, right? Can't wait to close the pages of this book and begin your grand adventure with God? After all, what's holding you back? . . .

God loves YOU.

YOU are his one-of-a-kind creation.

God wants to change the world with YOU right now.

You've seen how he uses ordinary, plain cheese pizza people (and some of us spicy pepperoni too).

You've seen the importance of keeping a real connection with God and seen the power of prayer.

You've seen how with God's help YOU can unplug from the headphones and cell phones so you can *hear* and *experience* the needs around you.

You've seen how God can chip away any hardness around your heart so YOU can *see* the needs around you.

You've seen how to get a team together to make a BIG difference.

You've seen how hospitality helps others and opens your heart.

You've begun to see the ways you can help.

Now it's time to get busy.

No matter your age, lack of funds, family circumstances, broken-out face, feelings of unpopularity, or anything else Satan tries to convince you is your downfall, you can still fulfill God's plan for you and make a permanent, positive difference in the world! And the world is waiting for what you can give.

The first Christians were told to spread the message about Jesus

first to their own communities,
then to nearby areas,
then to the whole world.

Do you have a three-part plan like that? Think about it. How can you show Jesus' love by helping more in your own family or among your closest friends? Who in your surrounding community (school, church, neighborhood, city) can you serve? Finally, where do you think God might take you that stretches you out of your comfort zone? Would you like to help orphans in Cambodia? Help the hungry in Kenya? Serve the poor in Bolivia?

You can make a three-part plan of action that gets you going. Here's an example of what you could do this week:

(Near) This week, I will _____ (pray, read my Bible every day, rake up the leaves in my elderly neighbor's yard, take my little brother out for ice cream).

(Far) This week, I will _____ (find out what programs local churches and ministries are doing in my area to see where I can volunteer).

(Farthest) This week, I will _____ _____ (go online to find organizations like World Vision who help children in other countries, and organize some friends to help me support a child in one of those countries).

30-HOUR FAMINE

One of World Vision's most popular programs for teens is the 30-Hour Famine, a worldwide movement of students who are serious about serving God and fighting hunger. For 30 hours, youth groups, student groups, individuals, and other groups give up eating—in order to experience what more than a billion people around the world go through every day. Before the 30-hour famine, participants raise funds to donate, do community service projects, tell people about what they will be doing, and draw attention to the needs of the poverty-stricken. It's a great way to introduce other teens to needs around the world, while helping to make a difference. World Vision provides a resource kit and plenty of activity and fund-raising ideas. Visit 30HourFamine.org or call 1-800-7FAMINE (1-800-732-6463).

Here are a few more ways you might make a difference. If you need to raise money for a great cause, try any of these:

➡ Have a garage sale and donate the profits. At the end of the day, you can also donate the items that don't sell!

➡ Set up a pet-walking service.

➡ Collect broken jewelry, and sell the gold.

➡ Have a combination car wash/bake sale.

➡ Hire yourself out to do odd jobs, babysitting, and yard work.

➡ Ask your school to have a Penny War for a local charity. The students put pennies in the teacher's jar they want to win and silver coins in the teacher's jar they want to lose.

➡ Decorate jars with a picture of your cause and ask permission to put them in local fitness centers, convenience stores, grocery stores, hair salons, doctor's offices, and so forth. Make sure you and your team can pick up donations once a week.

➡ Sell candy bars door-to-door, at school or youth group events (with permission), at your parents' offices, or to local businesses.

A good way to raise money is selling Current products to friends, neighbors, and family. This company has been around since 1950 and offers stationery, gift items, candy, and magazine subscriptions that you can sell. Collect the money up front, and, if you sell a certain number of items, you get to keep 50 percent of your sales (minus shipping). You can even send people to the company's Web site and make a profit when they place online orders. Visit CurrentFun.com.

If you still aren't sure what you can do to make a difference, here are some great ideas to get you going:

→ Lend a helping hand to neighbors, especially those who are elderly or sick, no matter what the season. In summer, offer to mow the yard a time or two. In fall, rake leaves. In winter, protect plants or shovel some snow. In spring, help plant a garden or pull some weeds.

→ Sit down and color a picture or play a game with your little brother or sister for at least thirty minutes today.

→ Write thank-you letters to your parents for all they have done for you. Leave them on their pillows.

→ Tell your teachers and youth leaders "thanks" for helping you learn.

→ Make a difference to your body, God's temple, by eating more fruits and veggies.

→ Start a Bible study at your house or school. Grab a few friends, some snacks, and dive in. Choose a book of the Bible to read together, and talk about what it means in your life.

→ Take a trash bag and pick up the litter along the roads in your neighborhood.

→ Ask your parents what three things you could do to make their lives easier this week. Do them!

→ Every time you find a penny, pray for someone who does not know Christ.

→ Start faithfully giving back to the Lord at least 10 percent of any money you get. Ask God to show you where he wants it to be used.

→ Start a garden project in your yard, neighborhood, school, or community. Plant vegetables and fruits that you can give to those in need.

→ Read stories of other teens making a difference. Learn from what they have done.

→ Learn how to write a press release. Ask your parents how to make a business call. With these skills, you can contact people in a professional manner, and you may be able to get your cause in the news.

→ Interview older people in your family. Video or audio record the interviews, or write them down so you can share your family's history and legacy of faith.

→ Call the local office of the Department of Children and Families to ask if there are homeless children in your area, and ask what they need the most. Then see what you and your friends can do to help.

→ Join Grammy Award-winning band Jars of Clay's mission to provide clean water to people in Africa. Take the forty-day water challenge. Drink nothing but water for the next forty days. Every time you would have bought a beverage, contribute the money to blood:water mission to build wells. Visit bloodwatermission.com.

→ Help Habitat for Humanity build houses for families
in need around the world. To actively build on a
Habitat site, you must be sixteen or older; however,
the ministry has programs for volunteers as young as five
years old. Habitat holds Youth Leadership Conferences,
an Act! Speak! Build! Week (a student-initiated week
of events to focus on ending poverty housing), campus
chapters (high school and college chapters that partner
with local Habitat for Humanity affiliates to educate,
build, and fund-raise), the Collegiate Challenge (a program
for students ages sixteen and older so they can spend
one break week building at a Habitat site in the United
States), Global Village (short-term build trips around
the country and the world for ages sixteen and up), the
Learn and Build Experience (a fun, hands-on experience
for high school students ages sixteen to eighteen to learn
about poverty issues and community), and Youth United
(a program for youth ages five to twenty-five who want
to raise money and help build a Habitat home in their
communities. The youth are the leaders, planners, press
agents, and fund-raisers for the home). Visit Habitat.org.

Now add your own! The possibilities are endless. God gave
you a creative mind, a body with hands and feet that can serve,
a vivid imagination, and a lot of smarts. What will you give back
to him?

JENNA

If you put down this book and make a list of people to help,
strategies to raise money, ways to contribute to the community,
that's good. BUT it's not the point of this book.

If you put down this book and make a list of people to help, strategies to raise money, ways to contribute to the community, AND actually accomplish the whole list, that's good. BUT it's still not the point of this book.

You can make list after list, do good works, be nice to parents, and even begin a successful global relief project at the age of twelve that feeds millions of children around the world and still find your life empty, still desire more, still miss the point of not only this book, but life.

Okay, Jenna, so what is the point?!!!
Glad you asked.

If I speak with human eloquence and angelic ecstasy but don't love, I'm nothing but the creaking of a rusty gate. If I speak God's Word with power, revealing all his mysteries and making everything plain as day, and if I have faith that says to a mountain, "Jump," and it jumps, but I don't love, I'm nothing. If I give everything I own to the poor and even go to the stake to be burned as a martyr, but I don't love, I've gotten nowhere. So, no matter what I say, what I believe, and what I do, I'm bankrupt without love. (1 Corinthians 13:1–3 MSG)

Paul makes it clear. If your first agenda is to change the world, then prepare to have a "bankrupt" heart. But if your first mission, before ANYTHING else, is to love, then get ready to outlive your life! The only way to love, I mean REALLY love, is to spend time getting to know the Creator of love—Jesus Christ. We can't love on our own.

"We love because he first loved us" (1 John 4:19 NIV).

Because he forgave you on the Cross, you can forgive. Because he conquered death, you can live forever. Because he lives, you can experience true life in relationship with him. Because he loves, you can love.

Have you gotten to know this love? Really? This love changes hearts, changes lives, changes the world. The only way you can change the world is through the heart-changing love of Jesus.

So spend some time with Jesus. Ask him to change you. Ask him to love through you. Then . . . THEN . . . you can make the difference you were designed to make.

We're cheering you on.
We're excited for you.

And we can't wait to see what YOU will do.

YOU were made to make a difference!

Random Acts of
Kindness and
Good Deeds

Include Your Own

How were you born to make a difference?

....

....

....

....

....

....

....

Do a **RAK**
(Random Act of
Kindness) often.

....

....

Collect food
for the local
food bank.

Get a group
together and
volunteer for local
nonprofit and
church-related
events.

Ask your principal for
permission to speak
to your student
body about a cause
in which they can
make a difference.

How were you made to reach out to others?

....

....

....

....

....

....

....

....

....

....

....

....

....

Make dinner or breakfast for your family.

HELP A FRIEND UNLOAD GROCERIES.

Find a nonprofit that provides coupons for its participants. Call the local newspaper and ask if they will donate the leftover coupon inserts from each Sunday's paper. Clip, organize, and donate the coupons to the nonprofit.

Help a neighbor weed her yard.

SMILE AT THE PEOPLE YOU MEET.

How do you want to change the world?

Take your sibling to the movies— just because.

Hold a Teddy Bear Drive and collect new stuffed animals for children who arrive at local shelters.

Hold the door open for someone.

Place a neighbor's newspaper on his doorstep.

NOTES

Chapter 1: Good Morning, Life
1. UNICEF, *The State of the World's Children 2009: Maternal and Newborn Health*, www.unicef.org/sowc09/report/report.php.
2. Ronald J. Sider, *Rich Christians in an Age of Hunger: Moving from Affluence to Generosity* (Nashville: Thomas Nelson, 2005), 10.
3. Ibid., 35.
4. Anup Shah, "Today, Over 25,000 Children Died Around the World," *Global Issues*, www.globalissues.org/article/715/today-over-25000-children-died-around-the-world.

Chapter 2: Plain Cheese Pizza
1. Telephone interview with Austin Gutwein, February 28, 2010.
2. Austin Gutwein and Todd Willard, *Take Your Best Shot: Do Something Bigger Than Yourself* (Nashville: Thomas Nelson, 2009).

Chapter 3: No Dropped Calls
1. Portio Research Mobile Factbook 2009. http://portioresearch.com. Accessed March 20, 2010.
2. Personal interview with Jessica Woolbright, December 14, 2009.

Chapter 4: Hidden Treasure
1. E-mail interview with Emily Richards, March 7, 2010.

Chapter 5: Unplug and Tune In
1. Hilary Le Cornu with Joseph Shulam, *A Commentary on the Jewish Roots of Acts* (Jerusalem: Netivyah Bible Instruction Ministry, 2003), 144.

2. Joe White and Larry K. Weeden, *Wired by God: Empowering Your Teen for a Life of Passion and Purpose* (Colorado Springs, CO: Focus on the Family, 2004).

3. Telephone interview with Leeland Mooring, March 8, 2010.

Chapter 6: 20/20

1. Telephone interview with Jeff Leeland, March 4, 2010.

2. Bill Gates Sr. with Mary Ann Mackin, *Showing Up for Life: Thoughts on the Gifts of a Lifetime* (New York: Broadway Books, 2009), 155.

Chapter 7: Stand Up for the Have-Nots

1. United Nations Development Programme, Human Development Report 2007/2008: *Fighting Climate Change: Human Solidarity in a Divided World*, 2007, 25, http://hdr.undp.org/en/reports/global/hdr2007–2008/chapters/, click on complete report.

2. *The Expositor's Bible Commentary with the New International Version of the Holy Bible* (Grand Rapids: Zondervan, 1990), 2:633–35.

3. Richard Stearns, *The Hole in Our Gospel* (Nashville: Thomas Nelson, 2008), 11.

4. Telephone interview with Zach Hunter, March 5, 2010.

5. United Nations World Food Programme, *WFP Facts Blast December 2009*, http://home.wfp.org/stellent/groups/public/documents/communications/wpf187701.pdf.

6. Anup Shah, "Today, Over 25,000 Children Died Around the World," *Global Issues*, www.globalissues.org/article/715/today-over-25000-children-died-around-the-world.

Chapter 8: When to Put Up Your Dukes

1. "How Teens Use Media," (June 2009), Nielsen. http://www.scribd.com/doc/16753035/Nielsen-Study-How-Teens-Use-Media-June-2009-Read-in-Full-Screen-Mode. Accessed March 2, 2010.

2. dc Talk and the Voice of the Martyrs, *Jesus Freaks: Stories of Those Who Stood for Jesus; the Ultimate Jesus Freaks* (Tulsa, OK: Albury Publishing, 1999), 208-9.

3. Homer, *The Iliad with an English Translation by A.T. Murray, Ph.D. in two volumes* (Cambridge, MA: Harvard University Press; London, William Heinemann, Ltd., 1924), 23.655–96.

Chapter 10: Hang Out Your Welcome Sign

1. "Teen Gets Carpal Tunnel from Texting," Ki Mae Heussner, http://abcnews.go.com/Technology/teen-carpal-tunnel-texting/story?id=10146773. Accessed June 28, 2010.
2. U.S. Bureau of the Census, *Poverty, 2007 and 2008; American Community Surveys*, 2, www.census.gov/prod/2009pubs/acsbr08-1.pdf.
3. Mark Nord, Margaret Andrews, Steven Carlson, *Household Food Security in the United States, 2008*, United States Department of Agriculture, iii, www.ers.usda.gov/Publications/ERR83/ERR83.pdf.
4. National and Community Service, "White House, USDA, National Service Agency, Launch Targeted Initiative to Address Hunger," www.nationalservice.gov/about/newsroom/releases_detail.asp?tbl_pr_id=1579.

Chapter 11: Blast the Walls Down

1. Rick Reilly, "There Are Some Games in Which Cheering for the Other Side Feels Better Than Winning," *Life of Reilly*, http://sports.espn.go.com/espnmag/story?section=magazine&id=3789373.
2. Hilary Le Cornu with Joseph Shulam, *A Commentary on the Jewish Roots of Acts* (Jerusalem: Netivyah Bible Instruction Ministry, 2003), 403.
3. Telephone interview with Alex Harris, March 3, 2010.
4. Alex Harris and Brett Harris, *Do Hard Things: A Teenage Rebellion Against Low Expectations* (Colorado Springs, CO: Multnomah, 2008); Alex Harris, Brett Harris, and Elisa Stanford, *Start Here: Doing Hard Things Right Where You Are* (Colorado Springs, CO: Multnomah, 2010).